EASY GUITAR
WITH NOTES & TAB

CHRISTMAS
FOR EASY GUITAR

T0083292

978-1-7051-7016-8

HAL•LEONARD®

For all works contained herein:
Unauthorized copying, arranging, adapting, recording, internet posting, public performance,
or other distribution of the music in this publication is an infringement of copyright.
Infringers are liable under the law.

Visit Hal Leonard Online at
www.halleonard.com

World headquarters, contact:
Hal Leonard
7777 West Bluemound Road
Milwaukee, WI 53213
Email: info@halleonard.com

In Europe, contact:
Hal Leonard Europe Limited
42 Wigmore Street
Marylebone, London, W1U 2RN
Email: info@halleonardeurope.com

In Australia, contact:
Hal Leonard Australia Pty. Ltd.
4 Lentara Court
Cheltenham, Victoria, 3192 Australia
Email: info@halleonard.com.au

STRUM AND PICK PATTERNS

This chart contains the suggested strum and pick patterns that are referred to by number at the beginning of each song in this book. The symbols ⊓ and ∨ in the strum patterns refer to down and up strokes, respectively. The letters in the pick patterns indicate which right-hand fingers play which strings.

p = thumb
i = index finger
m = middle finger
a = ring finger

For example; Pick Pattern 2
is played: thumb - index - middle - ring

Strum Patterns

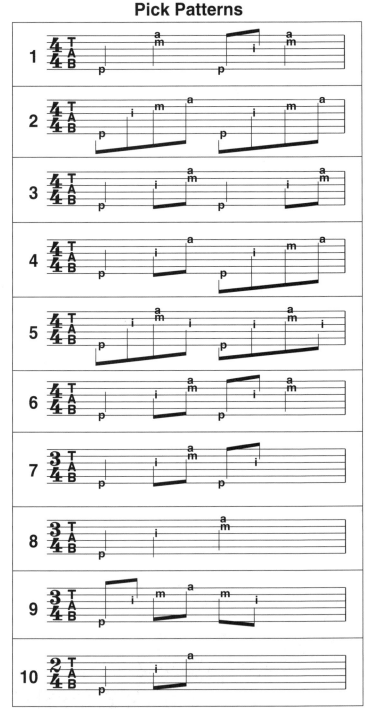

Pick Patterns

You can use the 3/4 Strum and Pick Patterns in songs written in compound meter (6/8, 9/8, 12/8, etc.). For example, you can accompany a song in 6/8 by playing the 3/4 pattern twice in each measure. The 4/4 Strum and Pick Patterns can be used for songs written in cut time (¢) by doubling the note time values in the patterns. Each pattern would therefore last two measures in cut time.

All I Want for Christmas Is You

Words and Music by Mariah Carey and Walter Afanasieff

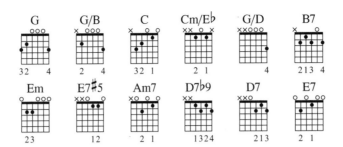

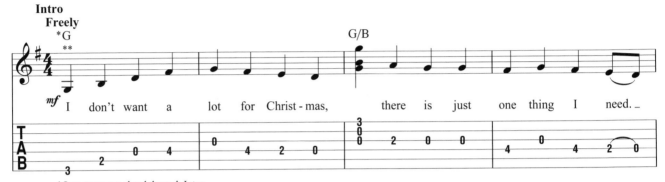

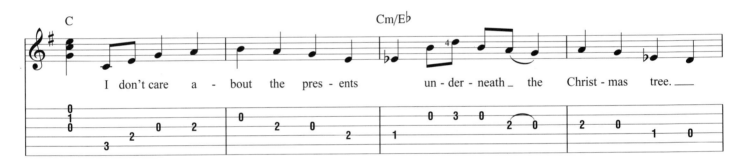

*One strum per chord through Intro
**Sung one octave higher throughout.

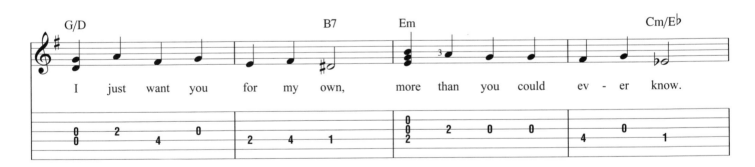

Copyright © 1994 UNIVERSAL TUNES, BEYONDIDOLIZATION, SONY MUSIC PUBLISHING (US) LLC,
TAMAL VISTA MUSIC and KOBALT MUSIC COPYRIGHTS SARL
All Rights for BEYONDIDOLIZATION Administered by UNIVERSAL TUNES
All Rights for SONY MUSIC PUBLISHING (US) LLC and TAMAL VISTA MUSIC Administered by
SONY MUSIC PUBLISHING (US) LLC, 424 Church Street, Suite 1200, Nashville, TN 37219
All Rights for KOBALT MUSIC COPYRIGHTS SARL Administered Worldwide by KOBALT SONGS MUSIC PUBLISHING
All Rights Reserved   Used by Permission

Strum Pattern: 3, 4
Pick Pattern: 3, 4

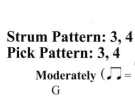

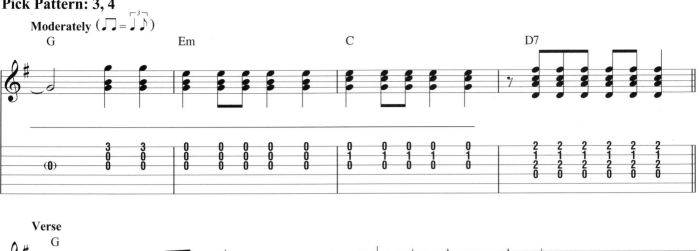

Verse

1. I don't want a lot ___ for Christ-mas, there is just one thing ___ I need. And
   I won't ask for much ___ this Christ-mas, I won't e - ven wish ___ for snow. ___ And

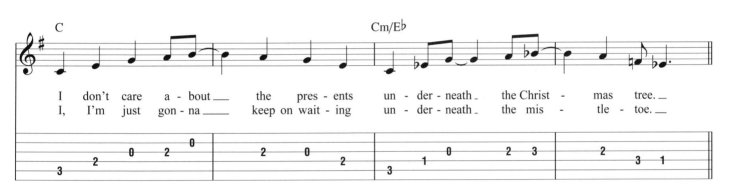

I don't care a - bout ___ the pres - ents un - der-neath ___ the Christ - mas tree. ___
I, I'm just gon - na ___ keep on wait - ing un - der-neath ___ the mis - tle - toe. ___

Verse

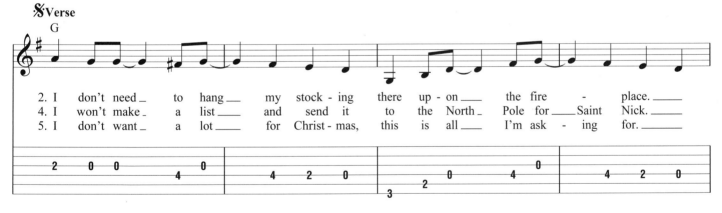

2. I don't need ___ to hang ___ my stock - ing there up - on ___ the fire - place. ___
4. I won't make ___ a list ___ and send it to the North ___ Pole for ___ Saint Nick. ___
5. I don't want ___ a lot ___ for Christ - mas, this is all ___ I'm ask - ing for. ___

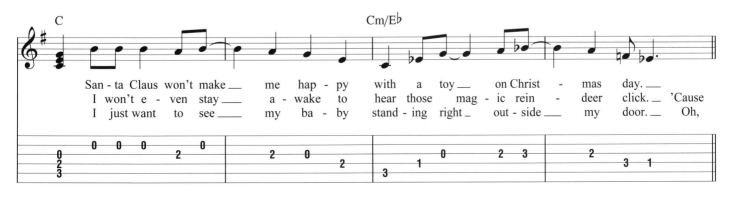

San - ta Claus won't make ___ me hap - py with a toy ___ on Christ - mas day. ___
I won't e - ven stay ___ a - wake to hear those mag - ic rein - deer click. ___ 'Cause
I just want to see ___ my ba - by stand - ing right ___ out - side ___ my door. ___ Oh,

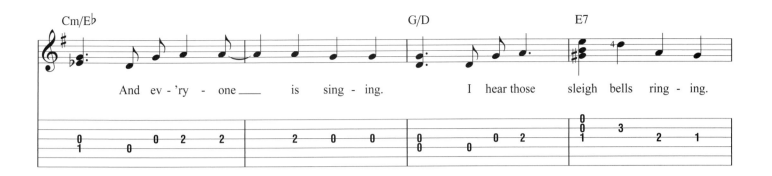

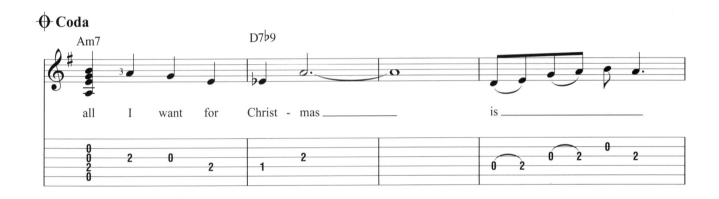

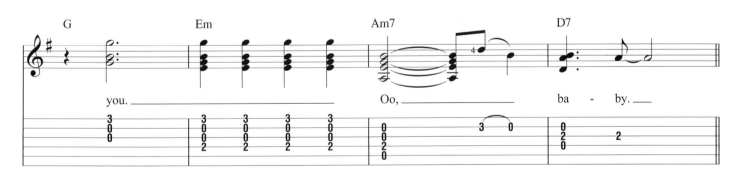

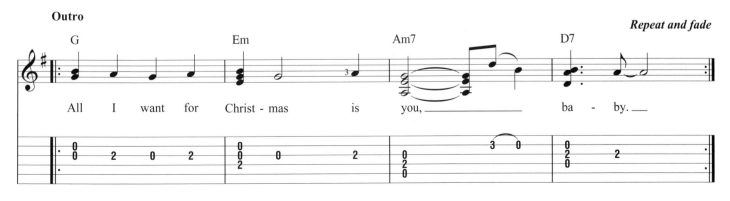

Blue Christmas

Words and Music by Billy Hayes and Jay Johnson

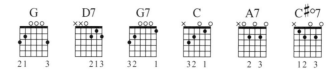

Strum Pattern: 2, 3
Pick Pattern: 3, 4

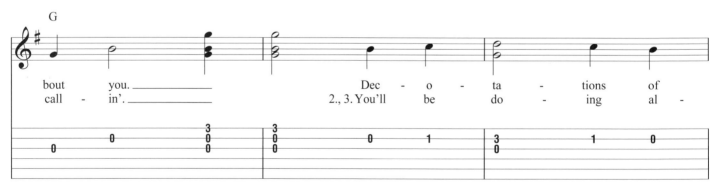

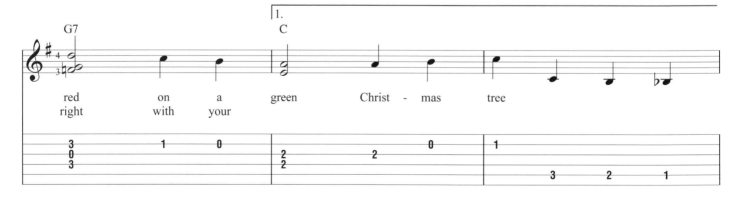

Copyright © 1948 UNIVERSAL - POLYGRAM INTERNATIONAL PUBLISHING, INC. and JUDY J. OLMSTEAD TRUST
Copyright Renewed
All Rights for JUDY J. OLMSTEAD TRUST Controlled and Administered by LICHELLE MUSIC COMPANY
All Rights Reserved   Used by Permission

won't be the same, dear, if you're not here with

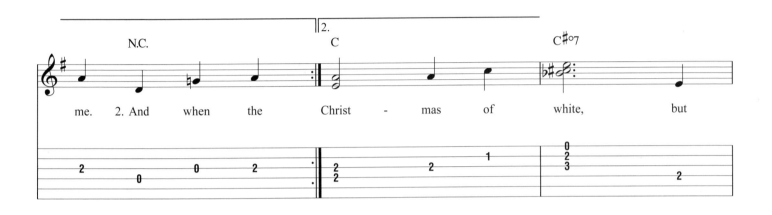

me. 2. And when the Christ - mas of white, but

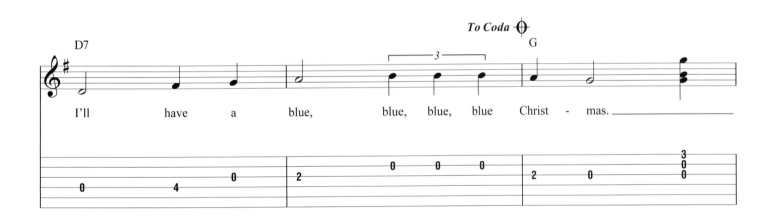

I'll have a blue, blue, blue, blue Christ - mas. _____

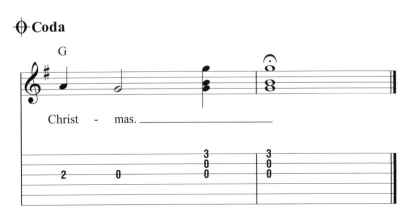

Christ - mas. _____

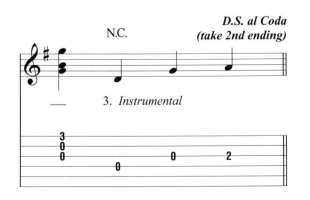

3. *Instrumental*

The Christmas Song
(Chestnuts Roasting on an Open Fire)

Music and Lyric by Mel Tormé and Robert Wells

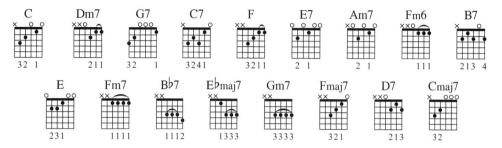

Strum Pattern: 2
Pick Pattern: 3

Verse
Moderately slow

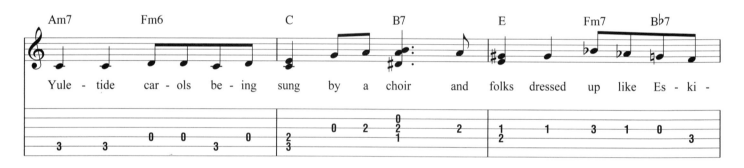

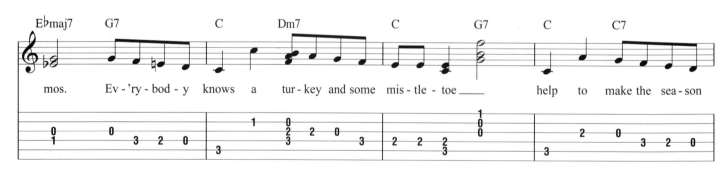

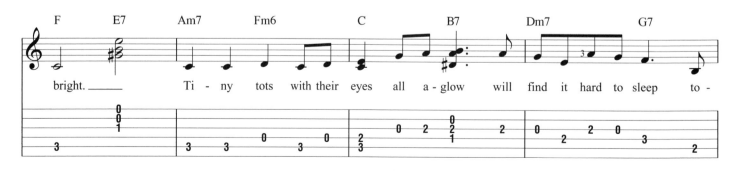

© 1946 (Renewed) EDWIN H. MORRIS & COMPANY, A Division of MPL Music Publishing, Inc. and SONY MUSIC PUBLISHING (US) LLC
All Rights on behalf of SONY MUSIC PUBLISHING (US) LLC Administered by
SONY MUSIC PUBLISHING (US) LLC, 424 Church Street, Suite 1200, Nashville, TN 37219
All Rights Reserved

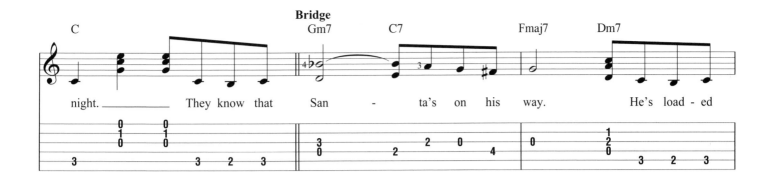

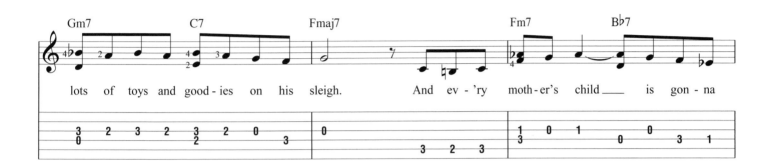

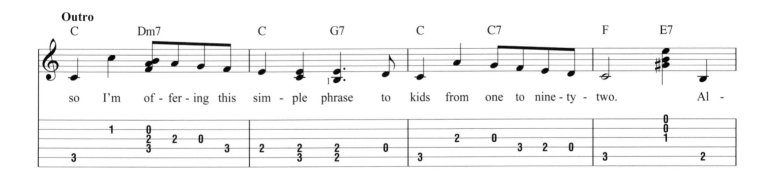

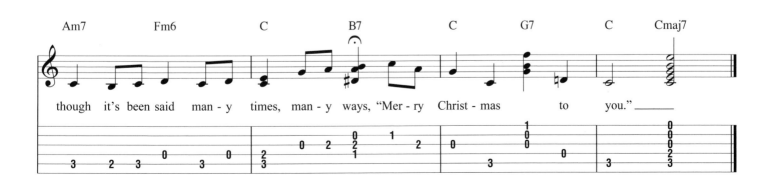

Christmas Time Is Here

from A CHARLIE BROWN CHRISTMAS

Words by Lee Mendelson
Music by Vince Guaraldi

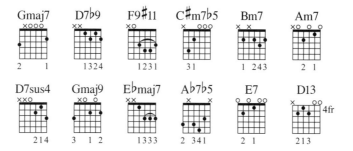

Strum Pattern: 7, 8
Pick Pattern: 7, 8

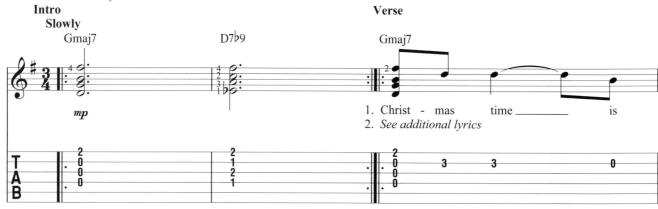

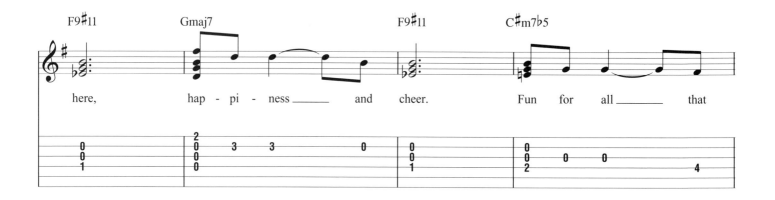

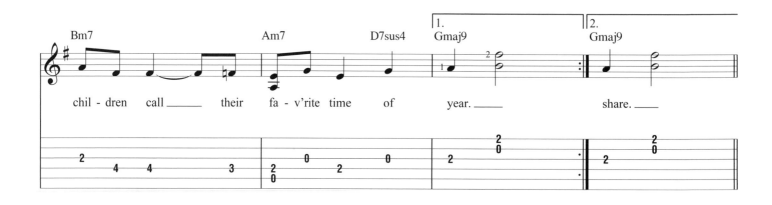

Copyright © 1966 LEE MENDELSON FILM PRODUCTIONS, INC.
Copyright Renewed
International Copyright Secured   All Rights Reserved

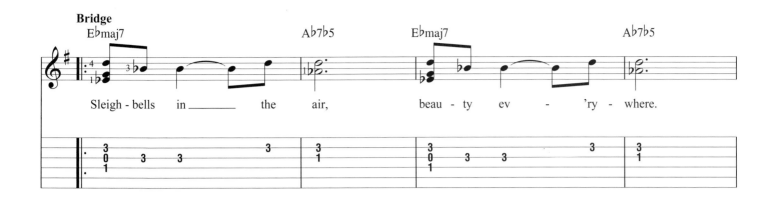

Sleigh - bells in _____ the air, beau - ty ev - 'ry - where.

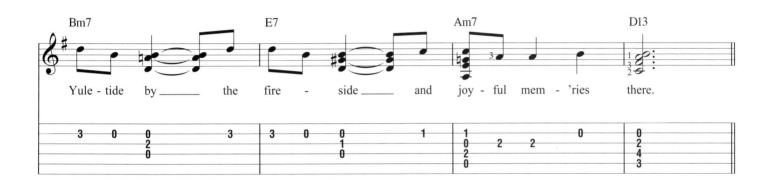

Yule - tide by _____ the fire - side _____ and joy - ful mem - 'ries there.

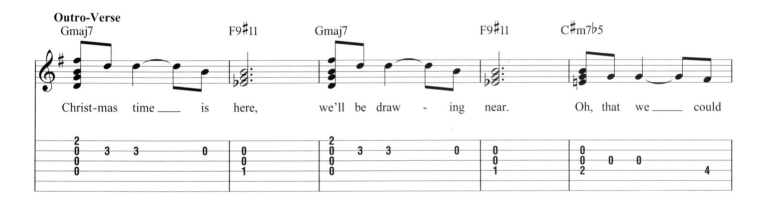

Christ-mas time ____ is here, we'll be draw - ing near. Oh, that we ____ could

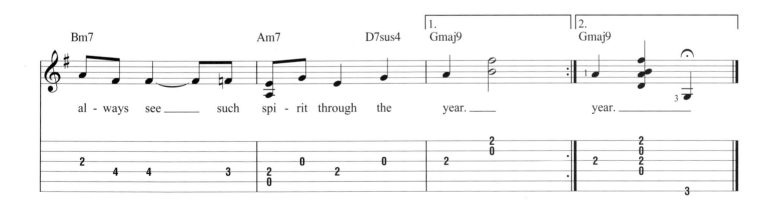

al - ways see _____ such spi - rit through the year. _____ year. _____

Additional Lyrics

2. Snowflakes in the air,
   Carols ev'rywhere.
   Olden times and ancient rhymes
   Of love and dreams to share.

Feliz Navidad

Music and Lyrics by José Feliciano

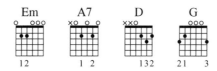

Strum Pattern: 1, 2
Pick Pattern: 2, 4

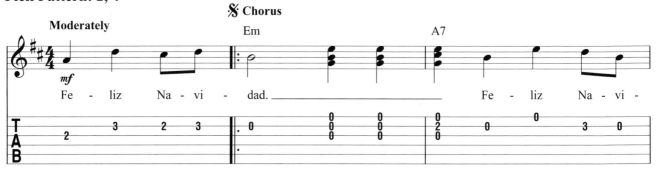

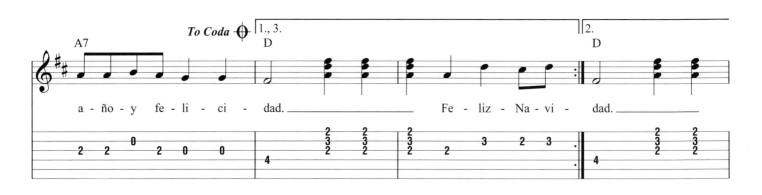

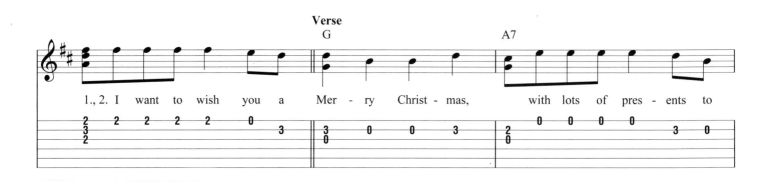

Copyright © 1970 J & H Publishing Company
Copyright Renewed
All Rights Administered by BMG Rights Management (US) LLC
All Rights Reserved   Used by Permission

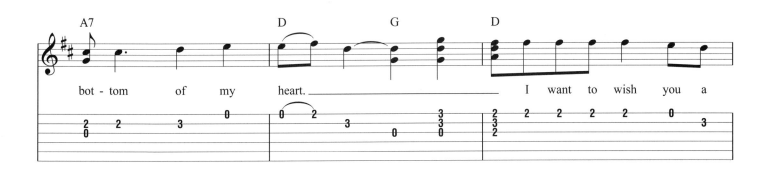

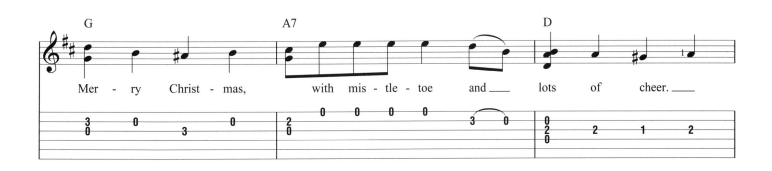

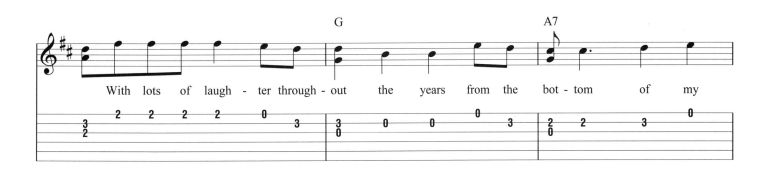

D.S. al Coda
(take repeat)

🔶 **Coda**

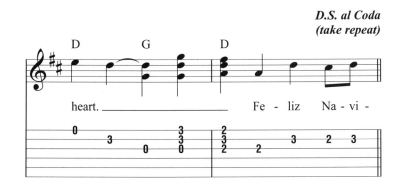

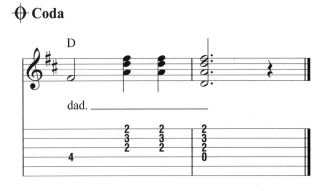

Frosty the Snow Man

Words and Music by Steve Nelson and Jack Rollins

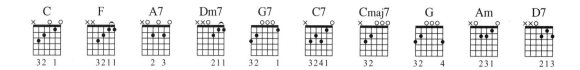

Strum Pattern: 2, 3
Pick Pattern: 3, 4

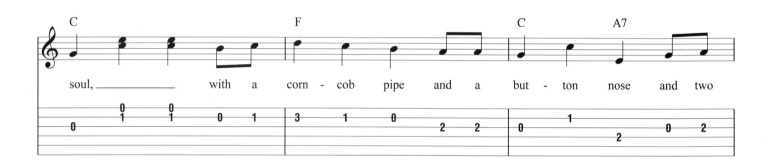

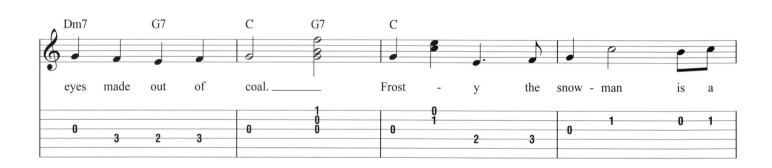

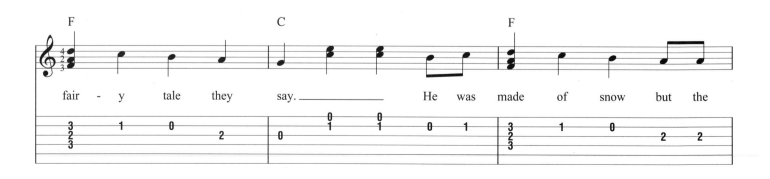

© 1950 (Renewed) CHAPPELL & CO., INC.
All Rights Reserved   Used by Permission

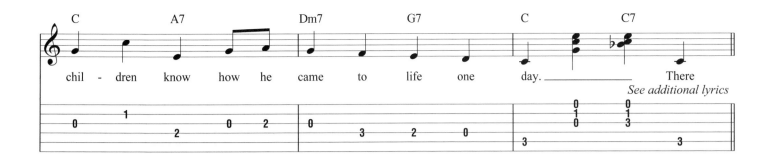

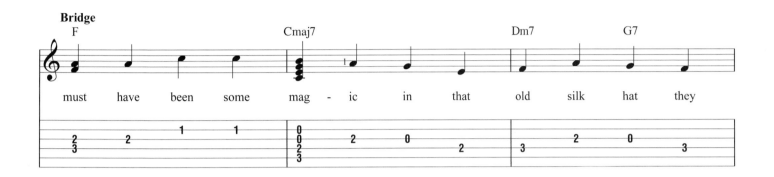

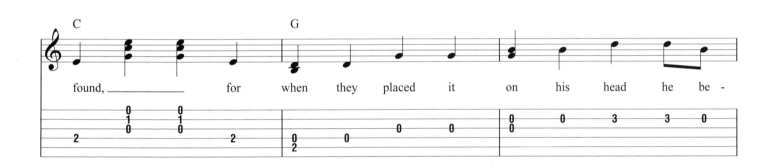

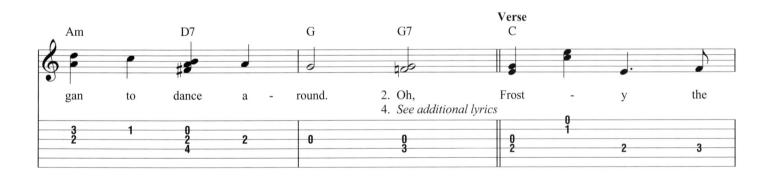

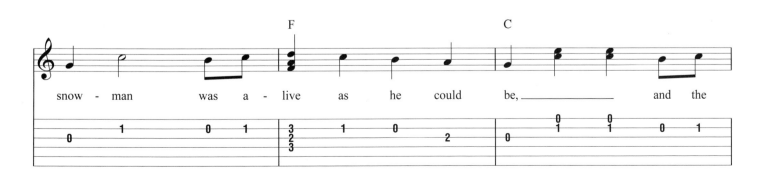

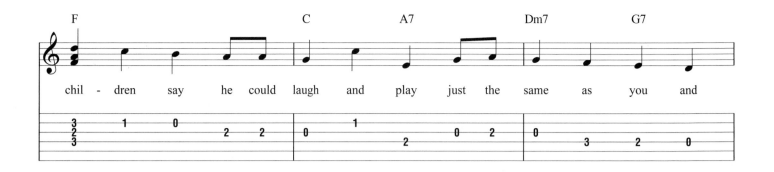

chil - dren say he could laugh and play just the same as you and

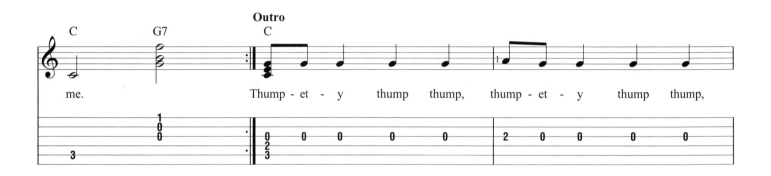

me. Thump - et - y thump thump, thump - et - y thump thump,

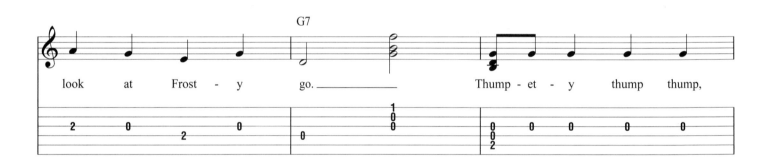

look at Frost - y go. Thump - et - y thump thump,

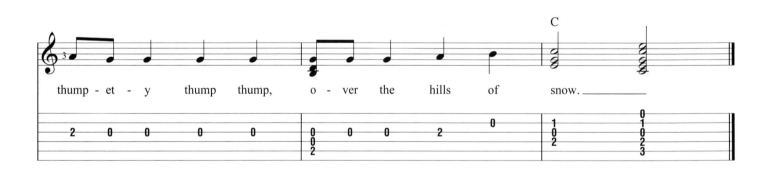

thump - et - y thump thump, o - ver the hills of snow.

Additional Lyrics

3. Frosty the snowman knew the sun was hot that day,
   So he said, "Let's run and we'll have some fun now before I melt away."
   Down to the village with a broomstick in his hand,
   Running here and there and all around the square, sayin', "Catch me if you can."

Bridge: He led them down the streets of town right to the traffic cop,
   And he ony paused a moment when he heard him holler, "Stop!"

4. For Frosty the snowman had to hurry on his way,
   But he waved goodbye sayin' "Don't you cry, I'll be back again someday."

Happy Holiday

from the Motion Picture Irving Berlin's HOLIDAY INN
Words and Music by Irving Berlin

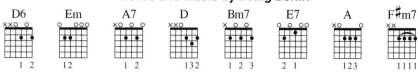

D6   Em   A7   D   Bm7   E7   A   F#m7

Strum Pattern: 2, 3
Pick Pattern: 3, 4

Verse
Slowly

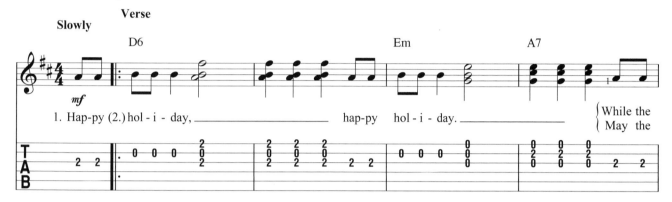

1. Hap-py (2.) hol-i-day, _____ hap-py hol-i-day. _____

{ While the
{ May the

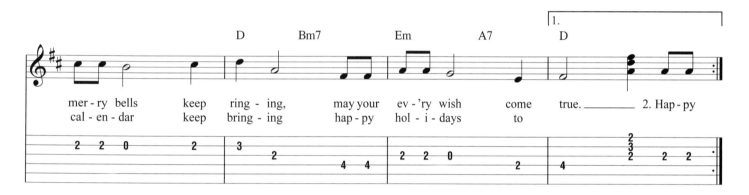

mer-ry bells keep ring-ing, may your ev-'ry wish come true. _____ 2. Hap-py
cal-en-dar keep bring-ing hap-py hol-i-days come to

2.

Verse

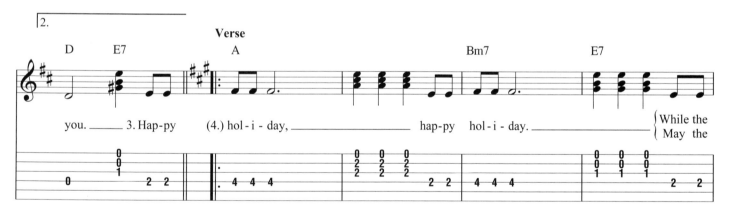

you. _____ 3. Hap-py (4.) hol-i-day, _____ hap-py hol-i-day. _____

{ While the
{ May the

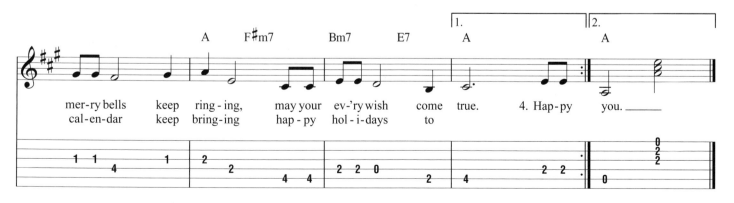

mer-ry bells keep ring-ing, may your ev-'ry wish come true. 4. Hap-py you. _____
cal-en-dar keep bring-ing hap-py hol-i-days to

© Copyright 1941, 1942 by Irving Berlin
Copyright Renewed
International Copyright Secured   All Rights Reserved

Happy Xmas
(War Is Over)
Written by John Lennon and Yoko Ono

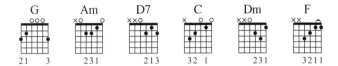

Strum Pattern: 8
Pick Pattern: 8

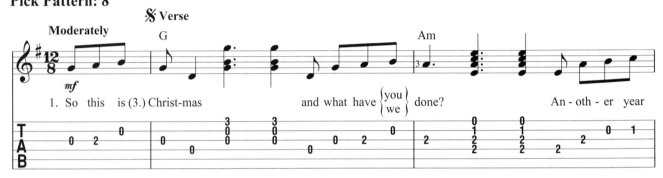

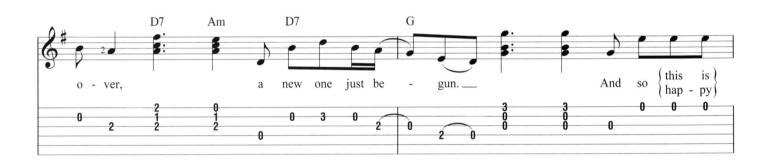

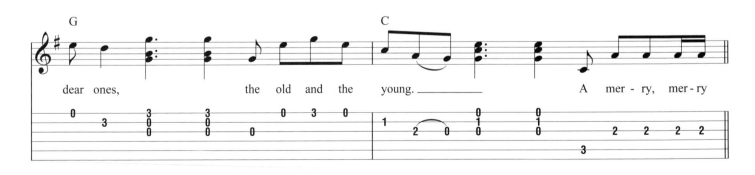

© 1971 (Renewed) LENONO MUSIC and ONO MUSIC
Administered in the United States by DOWNTOWN MUSIC PUBLISHING LLC
All Rights Reserved

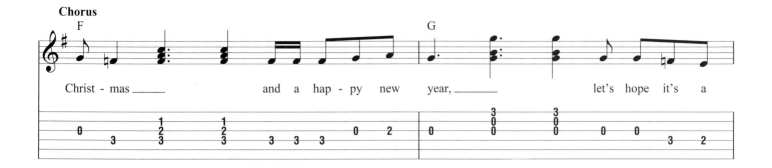

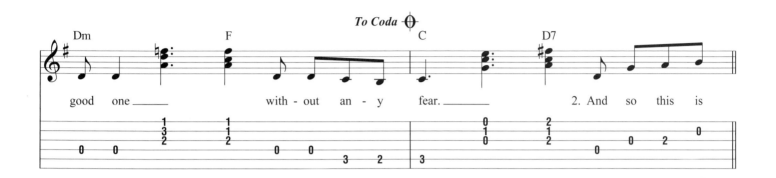

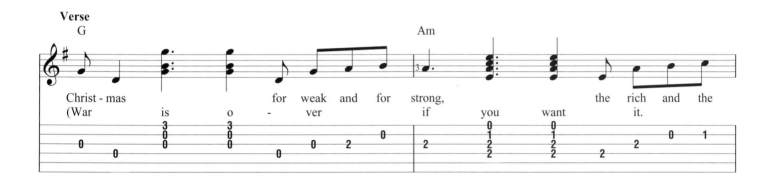

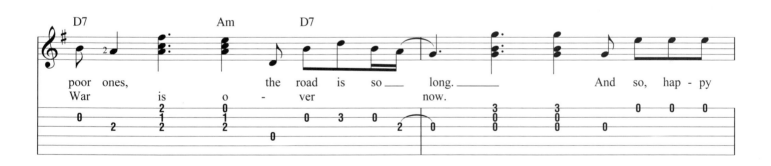

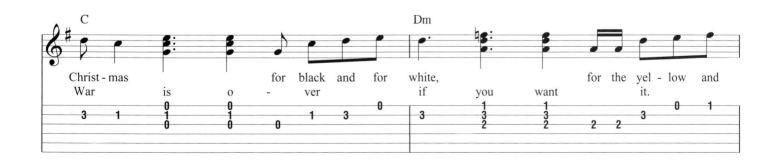

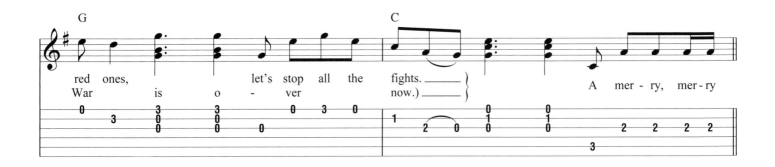

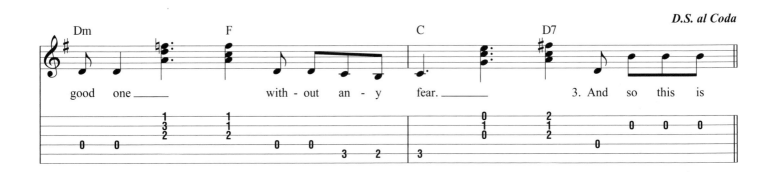

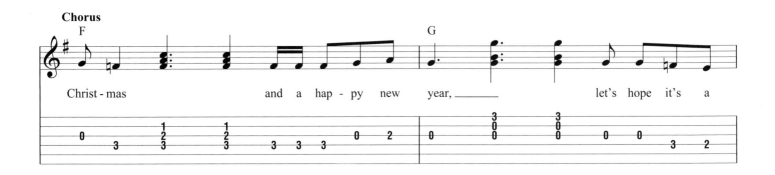

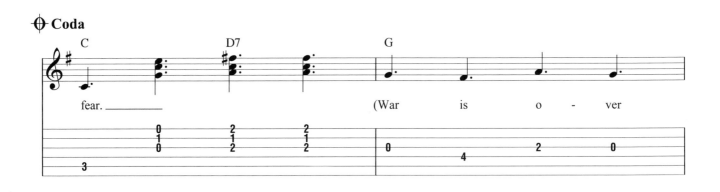

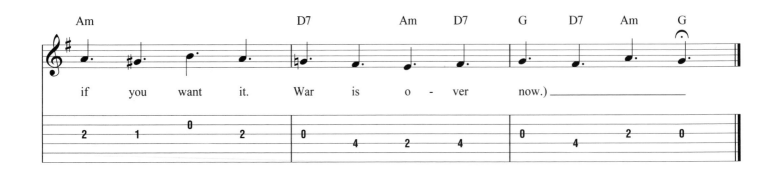

Have Yourself a Merry Little Christmas

from MEET ME IN ST. LOUIS

Words and Music by Hugh Martin and Ralph Blane

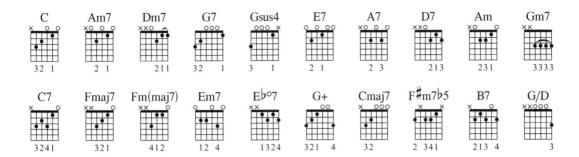

Strum Pattern: 4
Pick Pattern: 4

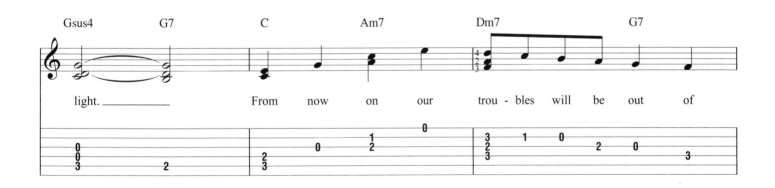

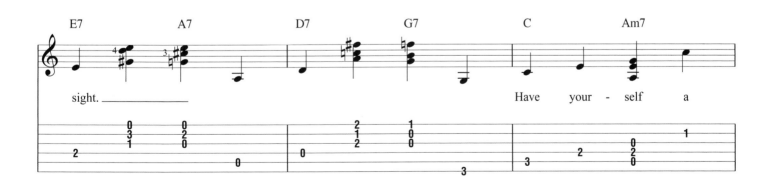

© 1943 (Renewed) METRO-GOLDWYN-MAYER INC.
© 1944 (Renewed) EMI FEIST CATALOG INC.
All Rights Controlled and Administered by EMI FEIST CATALOG INC. (Publishing) and ALFRED MUSIC (Print)
All Rights Reserved   Used by Permission

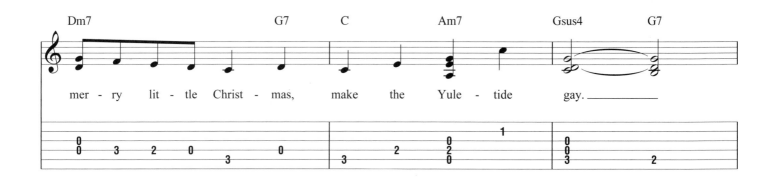

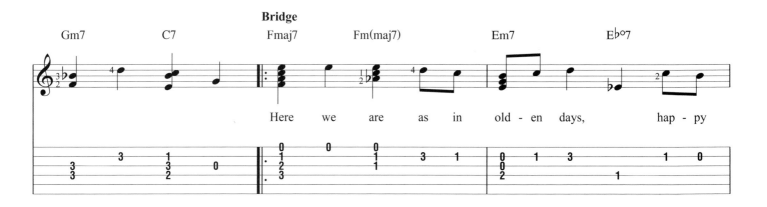

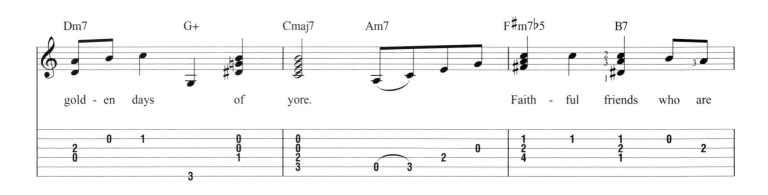

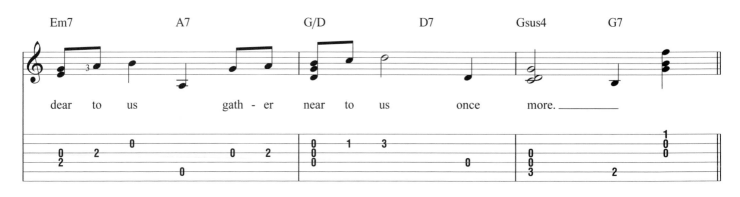

Here Comes Santa Claus
(Right Down Santa Claus Lane)

Words and Music by Gene Autry and Oakley Haldeman

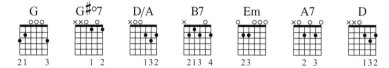

Strum Pattern: 4
Pick Pattern: 1

Intro
Moderately

Verse

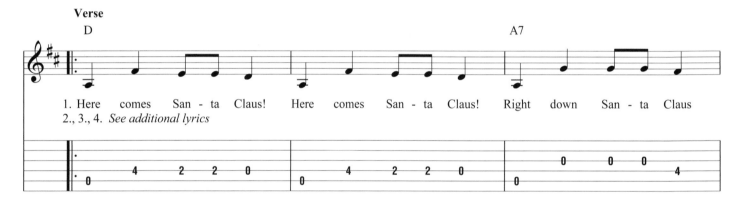

1. Here comes San-ta Claus! Here comes San-ta Claus! Right down San-ta Claus
2., 3., 4. *See additional lyrics*

Lane! Vix-en and Blit-zen and all his rein-deer are pull-ing on the

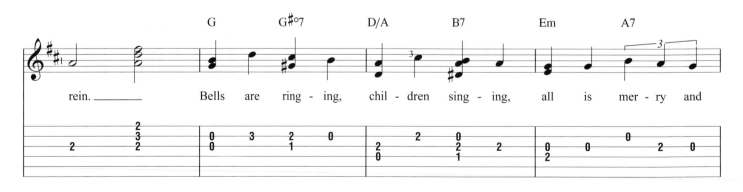

rein. _____ Bells are ring-ing, chil-dren sing-ing, all is mer-ry and

© 1947 (Renewed) Gene Autry's Western Music Publishing Co.
All Rights Reserved   Used by Permission

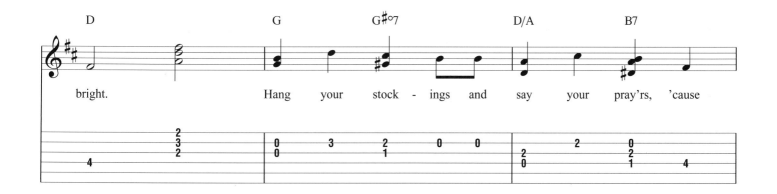

bright.   Hang   your   stock - ings   and   say   your   pray'rs,   'cause

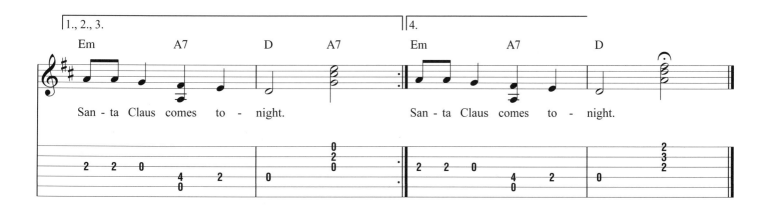

San - ta Claus comes to - night.   San - ta Claus comes to - night.

Additional Lyrics

2. Here comes Santa Claus! Here comes Santa Claus!
Right down Santa Claus Lane!
He's got a bag that is filled with toys
For the boys and girls again.
Here those sleigh bells jingle, jangle,
What a beautiful sight.
Jump in bed, cover up your head,
Santa Claus comes tonight.

3. Here comes Santa Claus! Here comes Santa Claus!
Right down Santa Claus Lane!
He doesn't care if you're rich or poor,
For he loves you just the same.
Santa knows that we're God's children;
That makes ev'rything right.
Fill your hearts with a Christmas cheer,
'Cause Santa Claus comes tonight.

4. Here comes Santa Claus! Here comes Santa Claus!
Right down Santa Claus Lane!
He'll come around when the chimes ring out;
Then it's Christmas morn again.
Peace on earth will come to all
If we just follow the light.
Let's give thanks to the Lord above,
Santa Claus comes tonight.

A Holly Jolly Christmas

Music and Lyrics by Johnny Marks

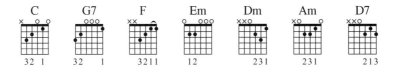

Strum Pattern: 2, 3
Pick Pattern: 3, 4

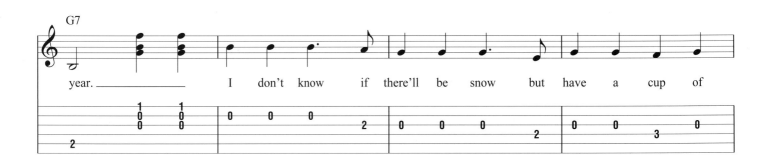

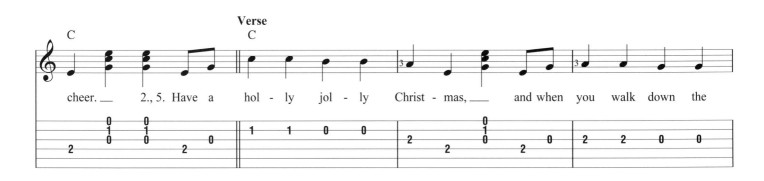

Copyright © 1962, 1964 (Renewed 1990, 1992) St. Nicholas Music Inc., 254 W. 54th Street, 12th Floor, New York, New York 10019
All Rights Reserved

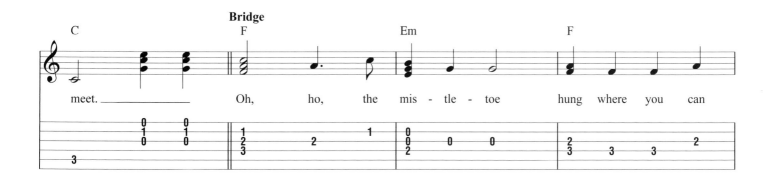

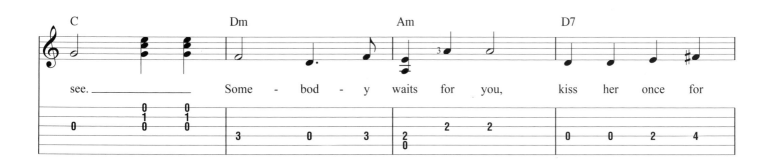

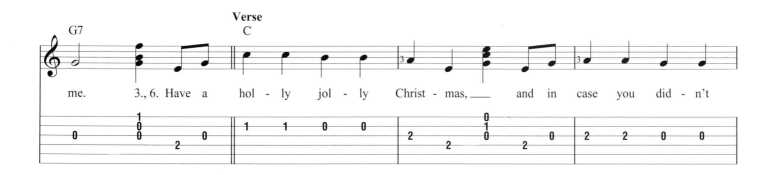

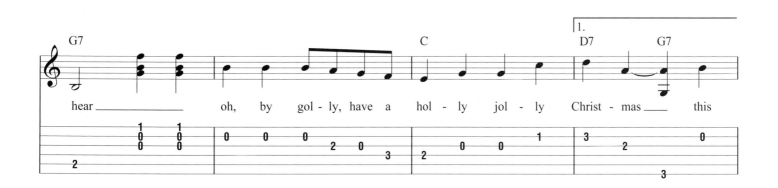

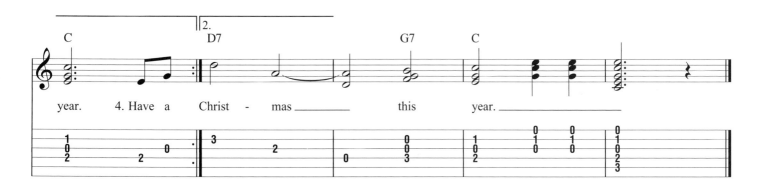

I Saw Mommy Kissing Santa Claus

Words and Music by Tommie Connor

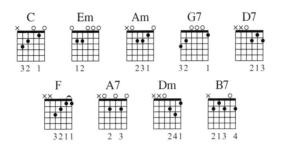

Strum Pattern: 2, 3
Pick Pattern: 3, 4

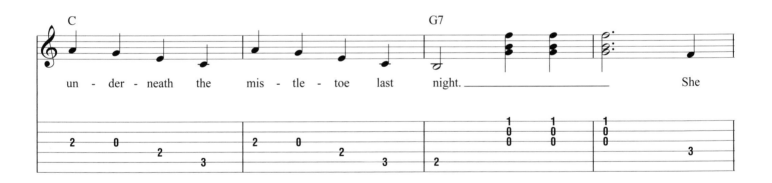

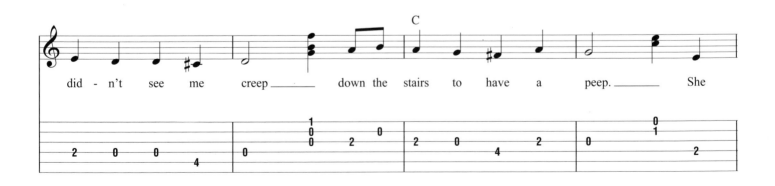

Copyright © 1952 by Regent Music Corporation (BMI)
Copyright Renewed by Jewel Music Publishing Co., Inc. (ASCAP)
International Copyright Secured   All Rights Reserved
Used by Permission

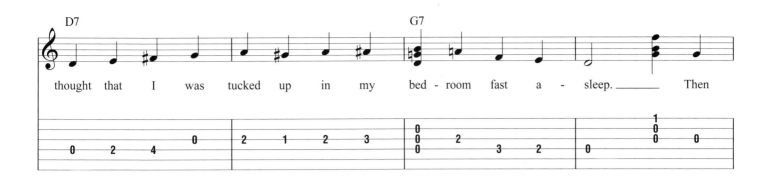

thought that I was tucked up in my bed - room fast a - sleep. _____ Then

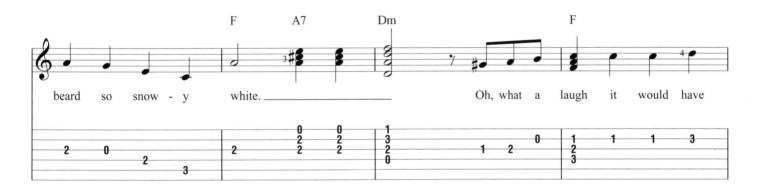

I saw Mom - my tick - le San - ta Claus, un - der - neath his

beard so snow - y white. _____ Oh, what a laugh it would have

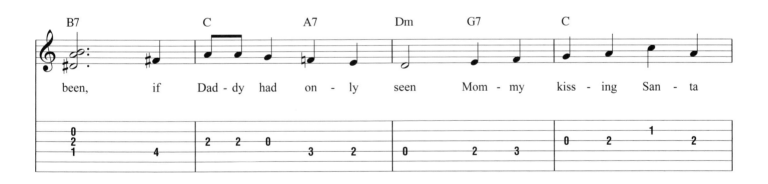

been, if Dad - dy had on - ly seen Mom - my kiss - ing San - ta

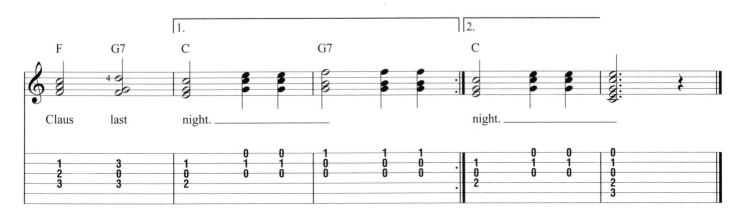

Claus last night. _____ night. _____

I'll Be Home for Christmas

Words and Music by Kim Gannon and Walter Kent

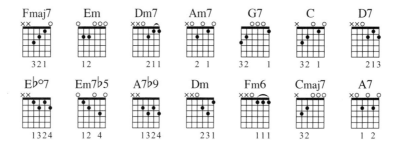

Strum Pattern: 3, 4
Pick Pattern: 3, 4

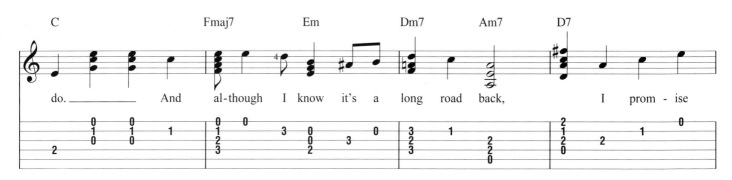

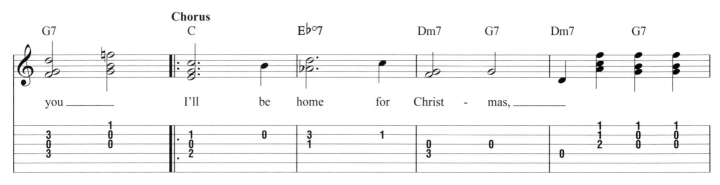

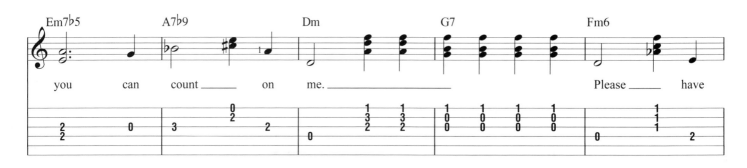

Copyright © 1943 (Renewed) by Gannon & Kent Music
All Rights Reserved   Used by Permission

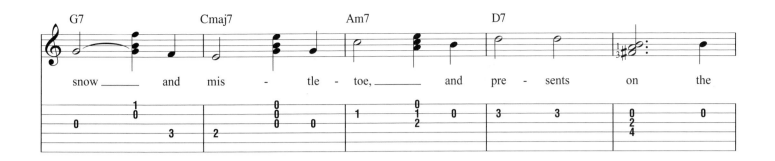

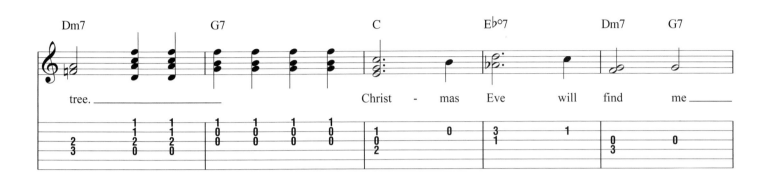

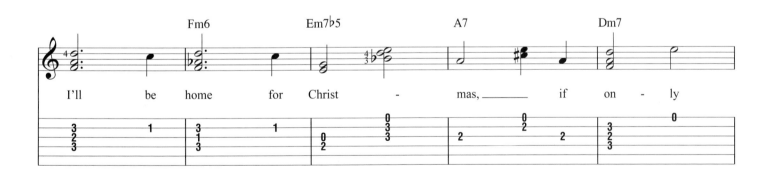

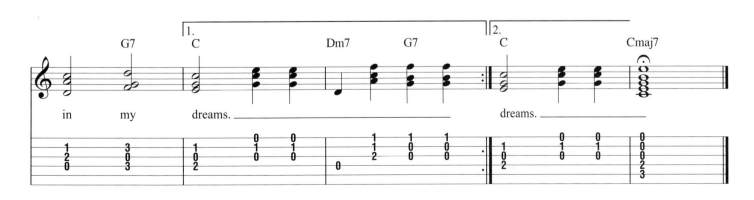

Jingle Bell Rock

Words and Music by Joe Beal and Jim Boothe

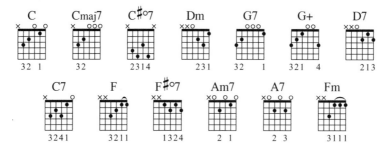

Strum Pattern: 1, 3
Pick Pattern: 2, 3

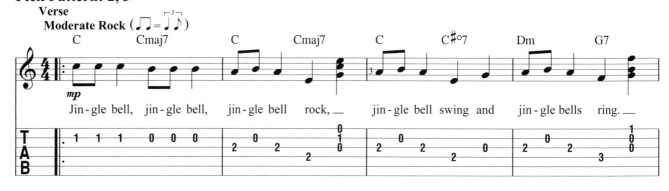

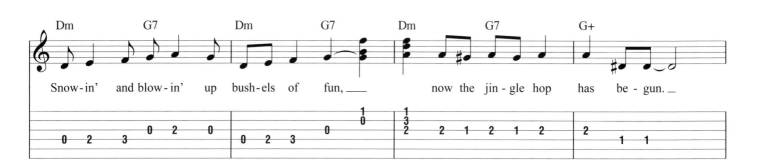

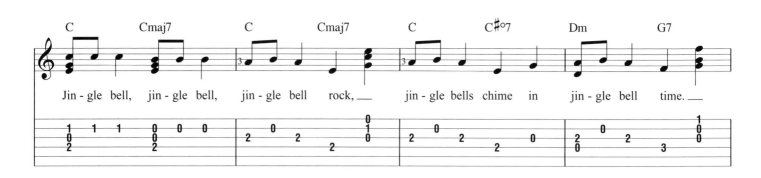

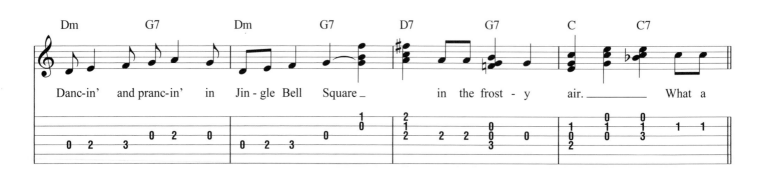

© 1957 (Renewed) CHAPPELL & CO., INC.
All Rights Reserved   Used by Permission

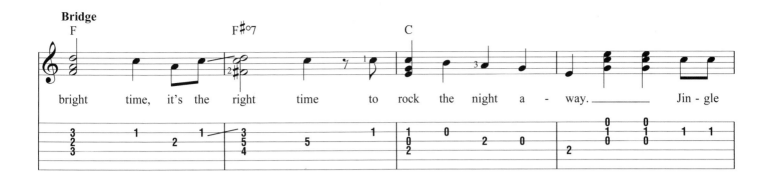

Bridge

bright time, it's the right time to rock the night a - way. _____ Jin - gle

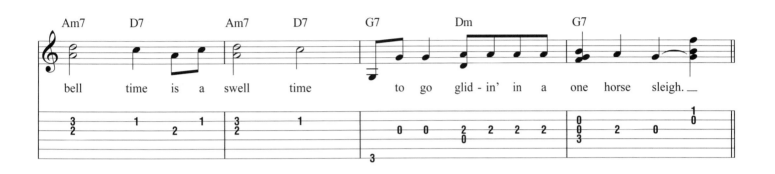

bell time is a swell time to go glid - in' in a one horse sleigh. __

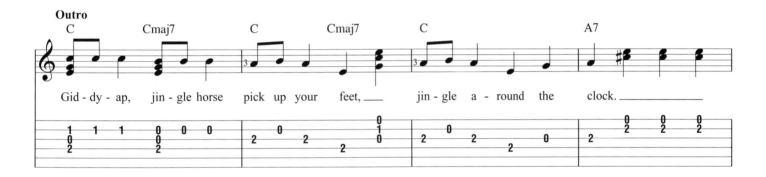

Outro

Gid - dy - ap, jin - gle horse pick up your feet, ____ jin - gle a - round the clock. _____

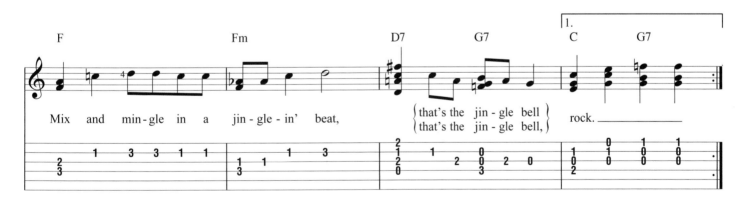

Mix and min - gle in a jin - gle - in' beat, { that's the jin - gle bell } rock. _____
{ that's the jin - gle bell, }

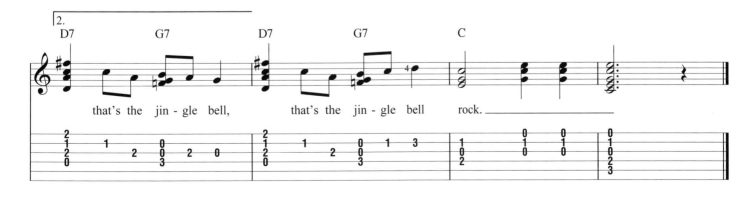

that's the jin - gle bell, that's the jin - gle bell rock. _____

Last Christmas

Words and Music by George Michael

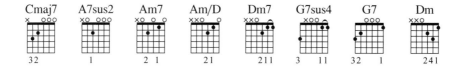

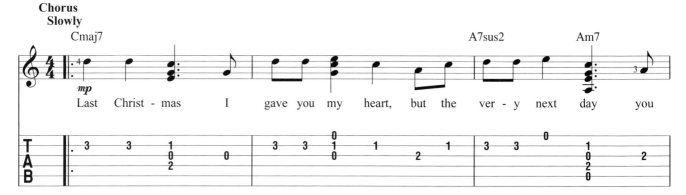

Strum Pattern: 6
Pick Pattern: 3

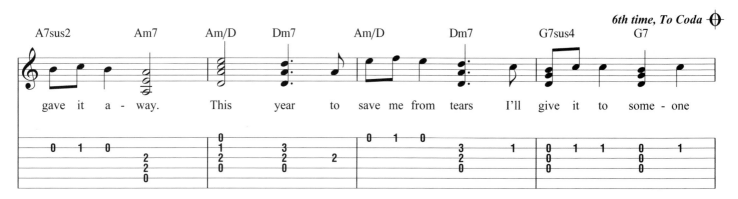

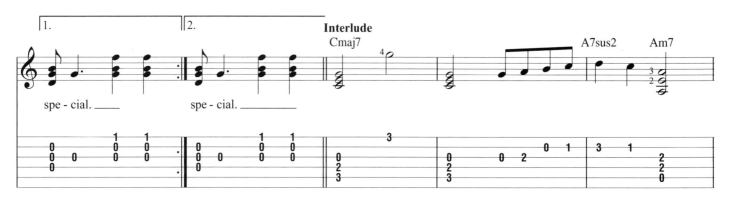

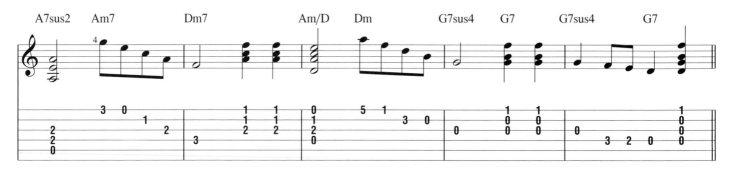

© 1984 WHAM MUSIC LIMITED
All Rights Administered by WC MUSIC CORP.
All Rights Reserved   Used by Permission

Verse

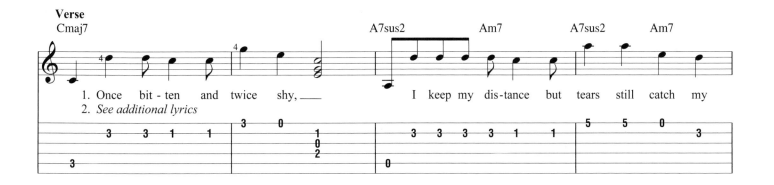

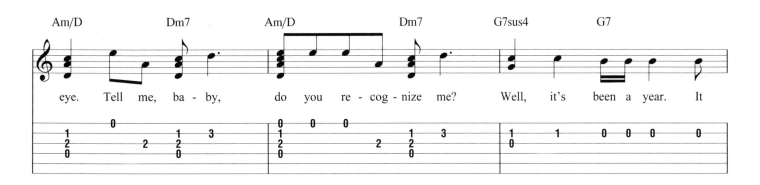

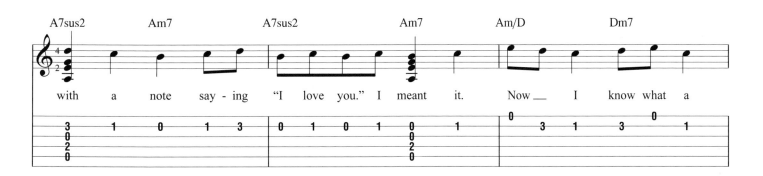

Additional Lyrics

A crowded room, friends with tired eyes.
I'm hiding from you and your soul of ice.
My God, I thought you were someone to rely on.
Me, I guess I was a shoulder to cry on.
A face on a lover with a fire in his heart,
A man undercover but you tore me apart,
Ooh, now I've found a real love.
You'll never fool me again.

Merry Christmas, Darling

Words and Music by Richard Carpenter and Frank Pooler

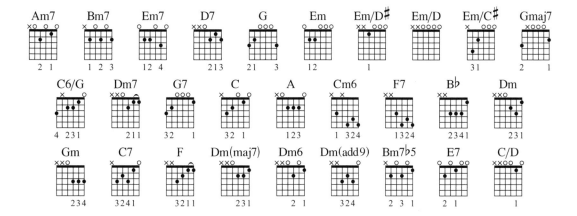

Strum Pattern: 4
Pick Pattern: 4

Intro
Freely

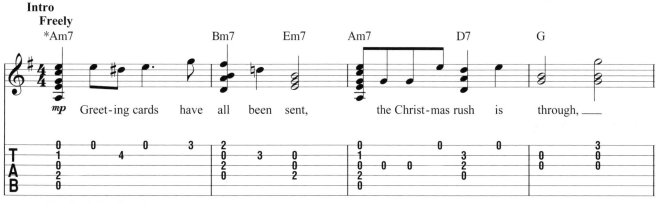

*Let chords ring throughout Intro

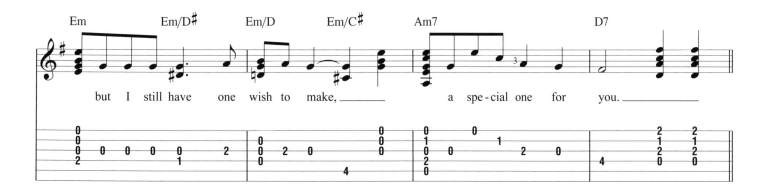

Verse
Moderately slow

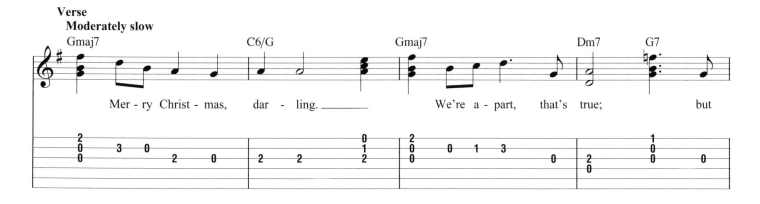

Copyright © 1970 IRVING MUSIC, INC.
Copyright Renewed
All Rights Reserved   Used by Permission

I can dream and in my dreams, I'm Christ - mas - ing with you.____

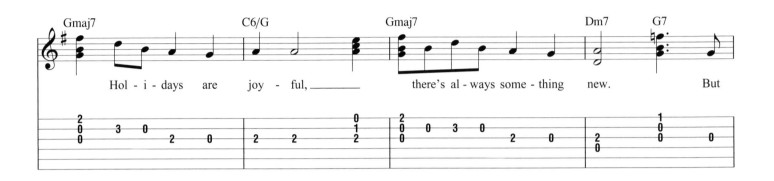

Hol - i - days are joy - ful,_____ there's al - ways some - thing new. But

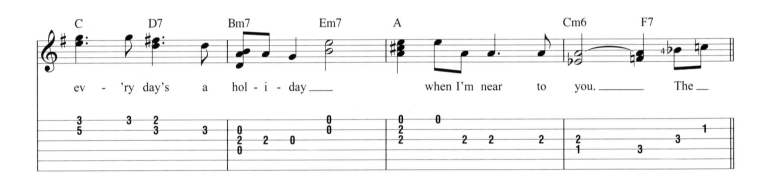

ev - 'ry day's a hol - i - day____ when I'm near to you.____ The__

§ Bridge

lights on my tree I wish you could see, I wish it ev - 'ry day._____ The

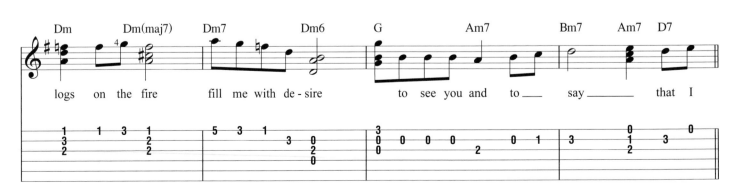

logs on the fire fill me with de - sire to see you and to__ say____ that I

Outro-Verse

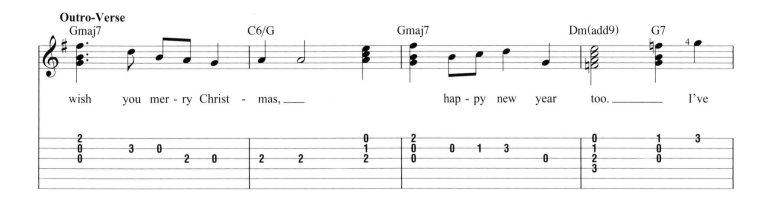

wish you mer - ry Christ - mas, ___ hap - py new year too. ___ I've

To Coda ⊕

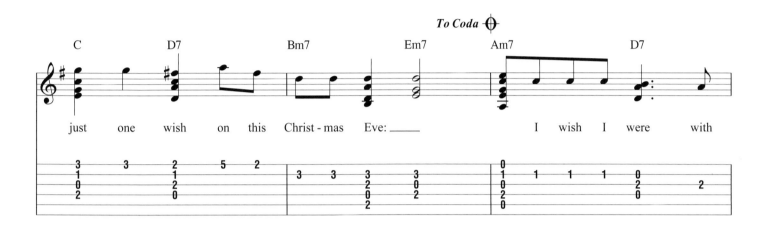

just one wish on this Christ - mas Eve: ___ I wish I were with

D.S. al Coda ⊕ **Coda**

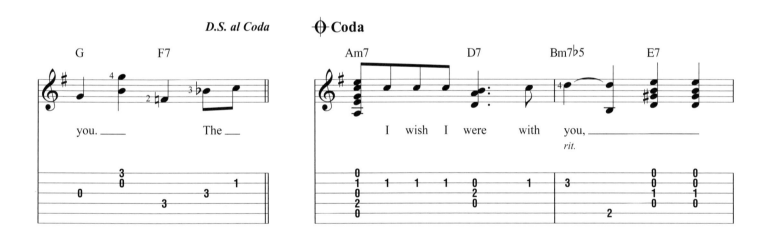

you. __ The __ I wish I were with you, _____
rit.

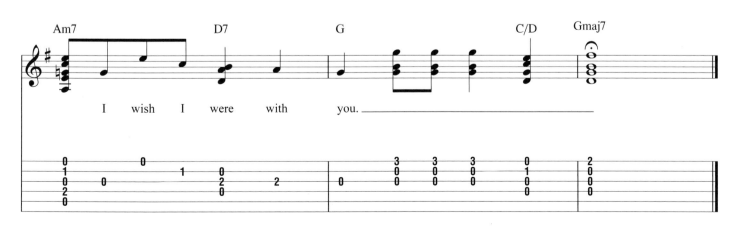

I wish I were with you. _____

Let It Snow! Let It Snow! Let It Snow!

Words by Sammy Cahn
Music by Jule Styne

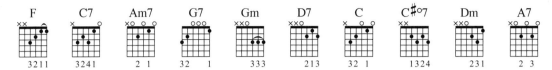

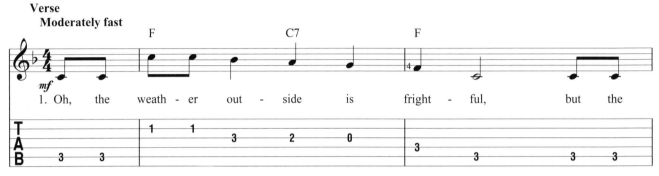

Strum Pattern: 2
Pick Pattern: 4

Verse
Moderately fast

1. Oh, the weath - er out - side is fright - ful, but the

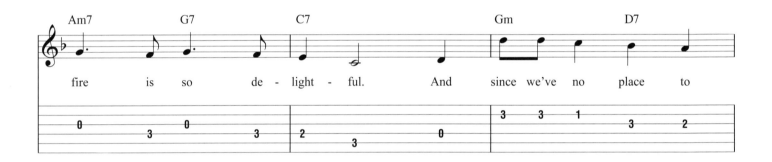

fire is so de - light - ful. And since we've no place to

go, let it snow, let it snow, let it snow! _____ 2. It

§ Verse

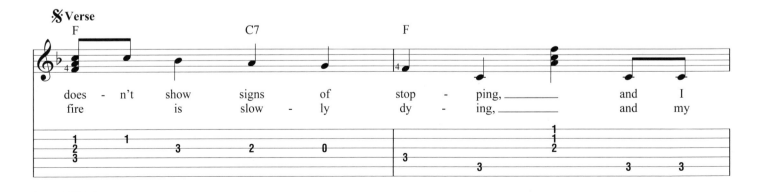

does - n't show signs of stop - ping, _____ and I
fire is slow - ly dy - ing, _____ and my

© 1945 (Renewed) PRODUCERS MUSIC PUBLISHING CO., INC. and CAHN MUSIC COMPANY
All Rights for PRODUCERS MUSIC PUBLISHING CO., INC. Administered by CHAPPELL & CO., INC.
All Rights for CAHN MUSIC COMPANY Administered by CONCORD SOUNDS c/o CONCORD MUSIC PUBLISHING
All Rights Reserved   Used by Permission

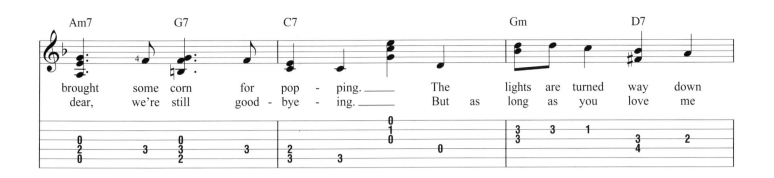

brought   some   corn   for   pop   -   ping._____   The
dear,   we're   still   good - bye   -   ing._____   But   as

To Coda ⊕

low,_____ ⎫   let   it   snow,   let   it   snow,   let   it   snow!_____   When   we
so,_____ ⎭

Bridge

fin - al - ly   kiss   good - night,_____   how   I'll   hate   go - ing   out   in   the

storm._____   But   if   you'll   real - ly   hold   me   tight,_____

⊕ **Coda**

D.S. al Coda

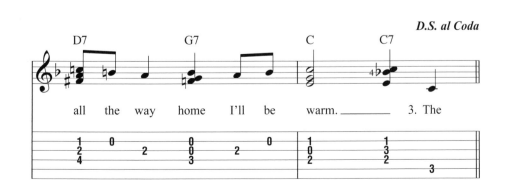

all   the   way   home   I'll   be   warm._____   3. The

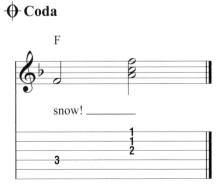

snow!_____

The Little Drummer Boy

Words and Music by Harry Simeone, Henry Onorati and Katherine Davis

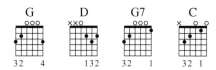

Strum Pattern: 3
Pick Pattern: 3

Verse
Moderately slow, in 2

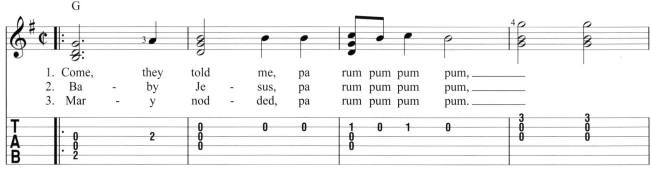

1. Come, they told me, pa rum pum pum pum, _____
2. Ba - by Je - sus, pa rum pum pum pum, _____
3. Mar - y nod - ded, pa rum pum pum pum. _____

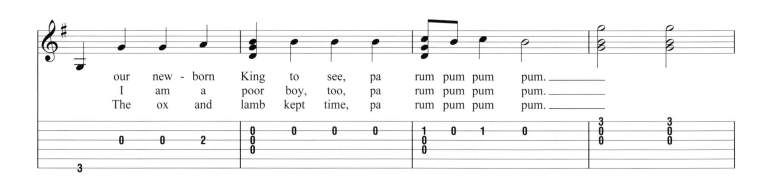

our new - born King to see, pa rum pum pum pum. _____
I am a poor boy, too, pa rum pum pum pum. _____
The ox and lamb kept time, pa rum pum pum pum. _____

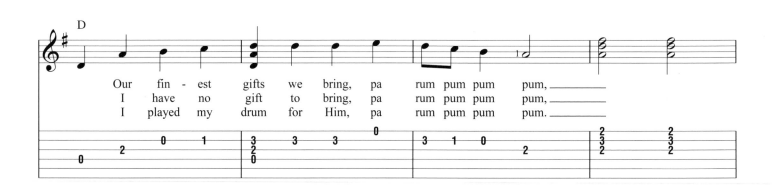

Our fin - est gifts we bring, pa rum pum pum pum, _____
I have no gift to bring, pa rum pum pum pum, _____
I played my drum for Him, pa rum pum pum pum. _____

© 1958 (Renewed) EMI MILLS MUSIC, INC. and INTERNATIONAL KORWIN CORP.
Worldwide Print Rights Administered by ALFRED MUSIC
All Rights Reserved   Used by Permission

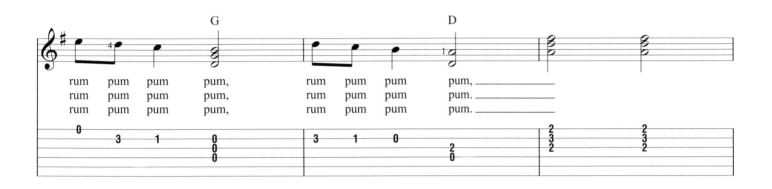

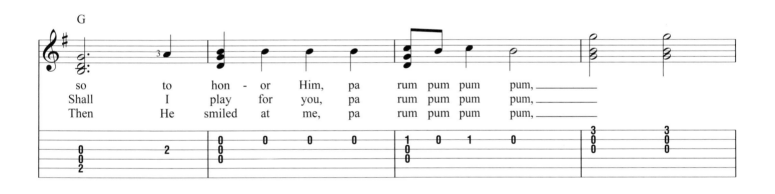

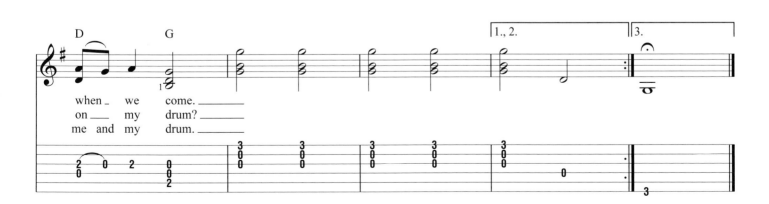

The Most Wonderful Time of the Year

Words and Music by Eddie Pola and George Wyle

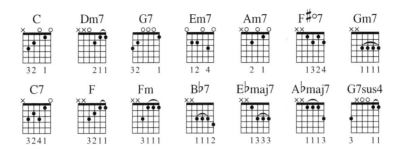

Strum Pattern: 7
Pick Pattern: 8

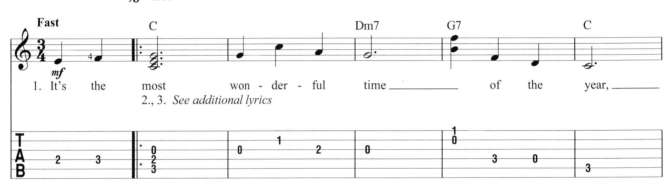

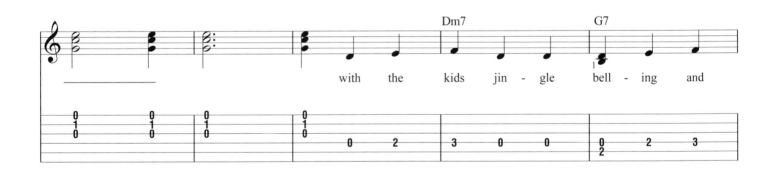

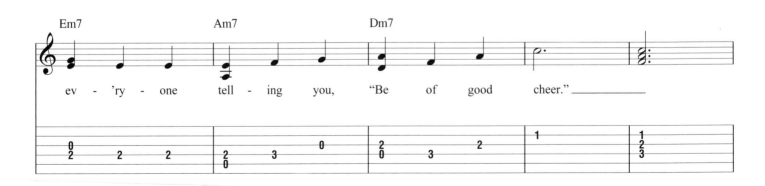

Copyright © 1963 Barnaby Music Corp.
Copyright Renewed
Administered by Lichelle Music Company
International Copyright Secured   All Rights Reserved

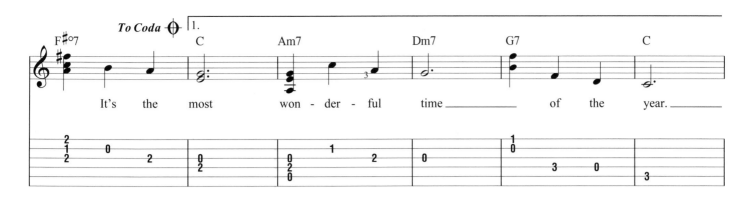

To Coda ⊕ |1.

It's the most won - der - ful time _____ of the year. _____

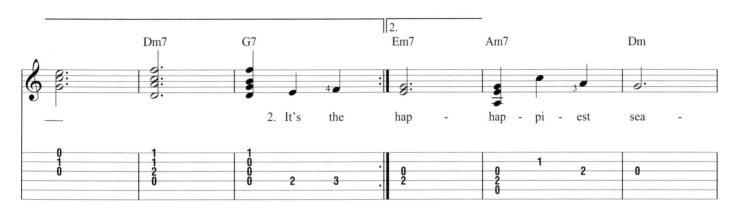

|2.

2. It's the hap - hap - pi - est sea -

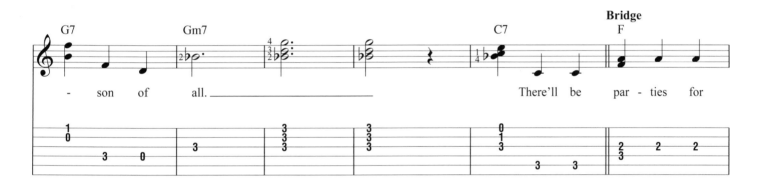

Bridge

- son of all. _____ There'll be par - ties for

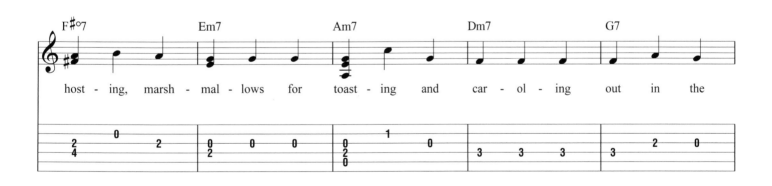

host - ing, marsh - mal - lows for toast - ing and car - ol - ing out in the

snow. There'll be scar - y ghost stor - ies and tales of the

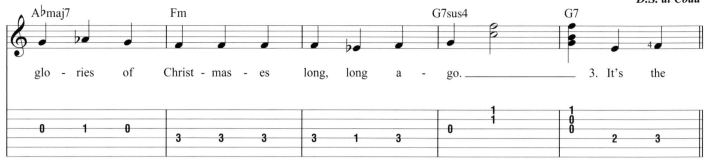

glo - ries of Christ - mas - es long, long a - go. _____ 3. It's the

Coda

most won - der - ful time, _____ it's the most won - der - ful

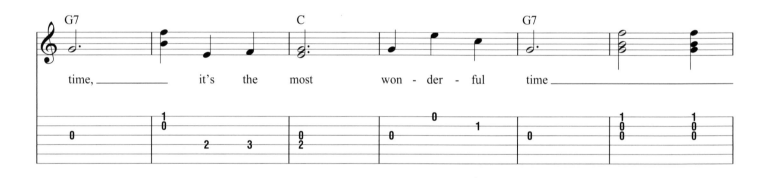

time, _____ it's the most won - der - ful time _____

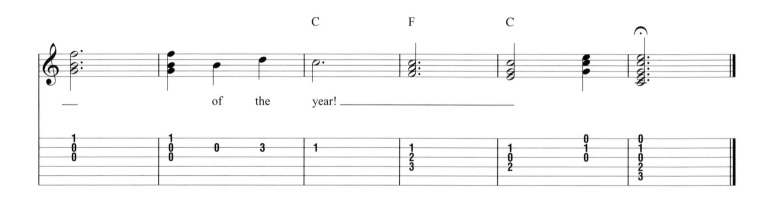

_____ of the year! _____

Additional Lyrics

2. It's the hap-happiest season of all,
With those holiday greetings
And gay happy meetings
When friends come to call.
It's the hap-piest season of all.

3. It's the most wonderful time of the year.
There'll be much mistletoeing
And hearts will be glowing
When loved ones are near.
It's the most wonderful time,
It's the most wonderful time,
It's the most wonderful time of the year!

My Favorite Things

from THE SOUND OF MUSIC

Lyrics by Oscar Hammerstein II
Music by Richard Rodgers

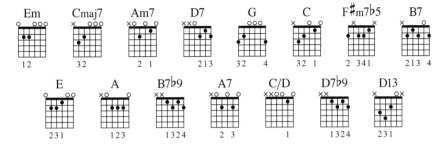

Em   Cmaj7   Am7   D7   G   C   F#m7♭5   B7

E   A   B7♭9   A7   C/D   D7♭9   D13

Strum Pattern: 8
Pick Pattern: 8

Verse
Fast

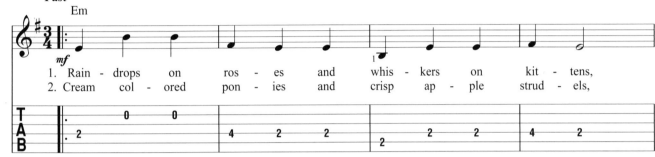

Em

mf

1. Rain - drops on ros - es and whis - kers on kit - tens,
2. Cream col - ored pon - ies and crisp ap - ple strud - els,

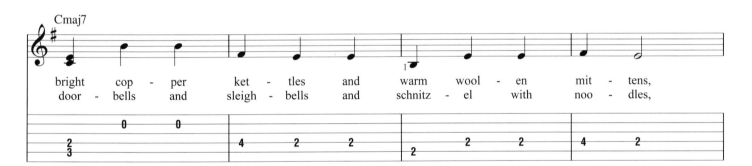

Cmaj7

bright cop - per ket - tles and warm wool - en mit - tens,
door - bells and sleigh - bells and schnitz - el with noo - dles,

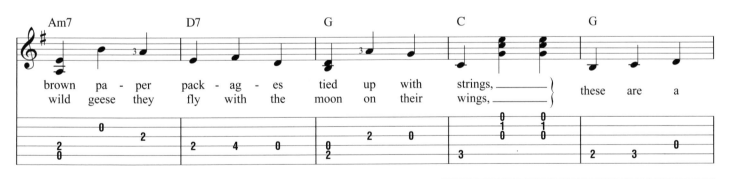

Am7   D7   G   C   G

brown pa - per pack - ag - es tied up with strings, these are a
wild geese they fly with the moon on with their wings,

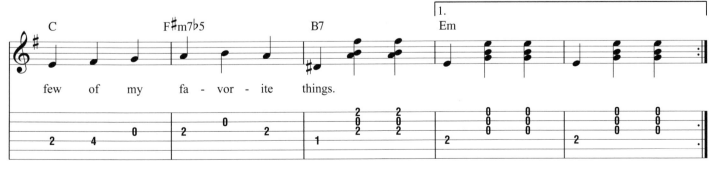

C   F#m7♭5   B7   Em

1.

few of my fa - vor - ite things.

Copyright © 1959 Williamson Music Company c/o Concord Music Publishing
Copyright Renewed
All Rights Reserved   Used by Permission

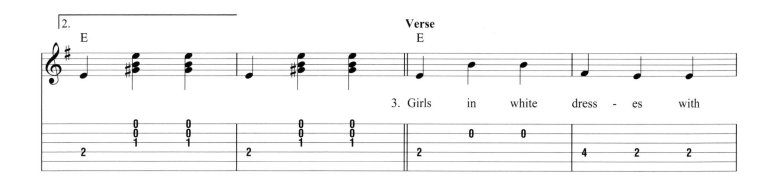

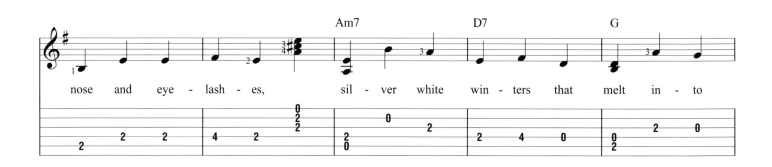

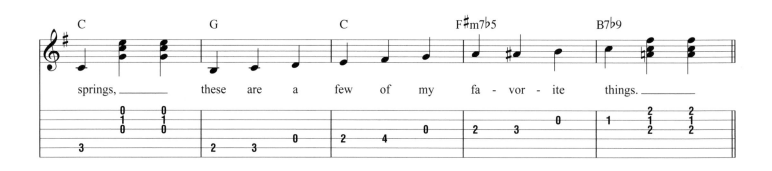

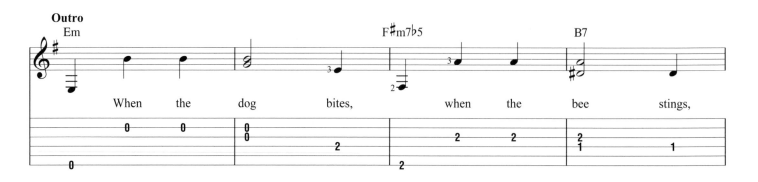

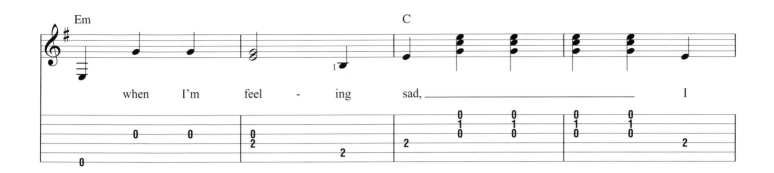

when I'm feel - ing sad, _____ I

sim - ply re - mem - ber my fa - vor - ite things and

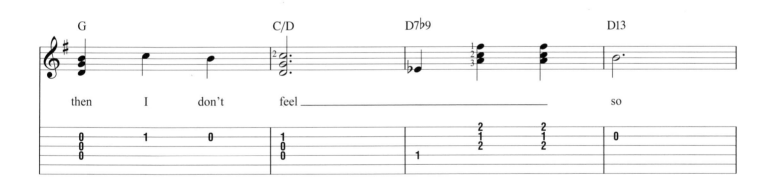

then I don't feel _____ so

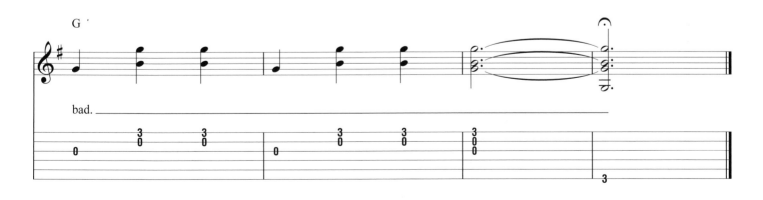

bad. _____

Rockin' Around the Christmas Tree

Music and Lyrics by Johnny Marks

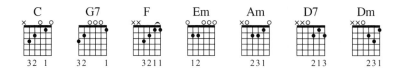

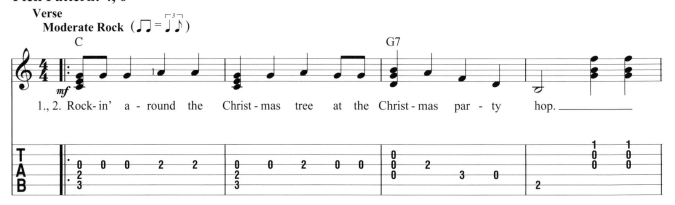

Strum Pattern: 2, 6
Pick Pattern: 4, 6

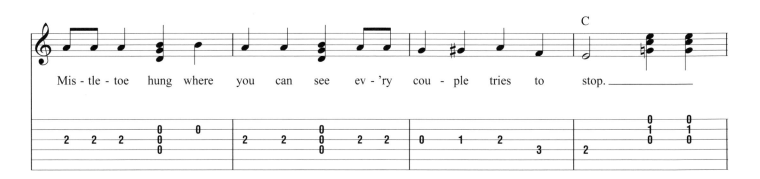

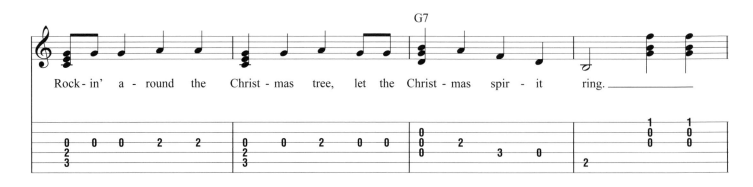

Copyright © 1958 (Renewed 1986) St. Nicholas Music Inc., 254 W. 54th Street, 12th Floor, New York, New York 10019
All Rights Reserved

Bridge

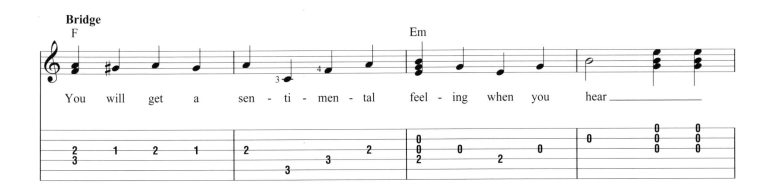

You will get a sen - ti - men - tal feel - ing when you hear ____

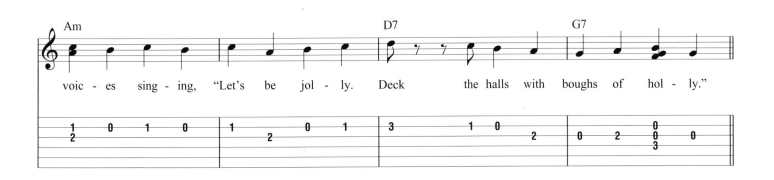

voic - es sing - ing, "Let's be jol - ly. Deck the halls with boughs of hol - ly."

Outro-Verse

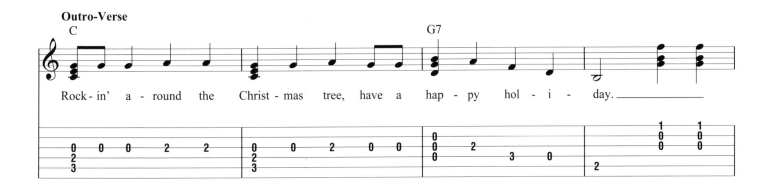

Rock - in' a - round the Christ - mas tree, have a hap - py hol - i - day. ____

Ev - 'ry - one danc - ing mer - ri - ly in the new old - fash - ioned way. ____

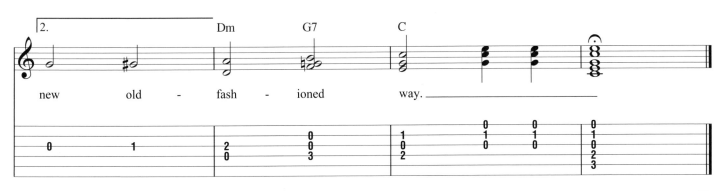

new old - fash - ioned way. ____

Rudolph the Red-Nosed Reindeer

Music and Lyrics by Johnny Marks

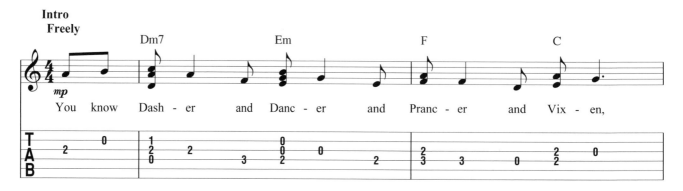

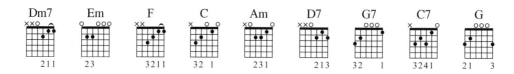

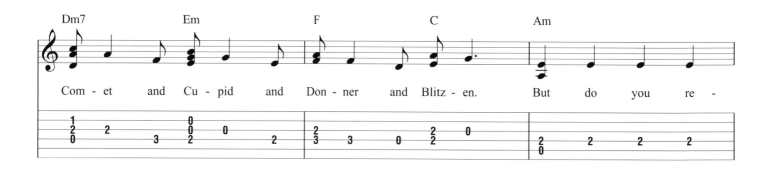

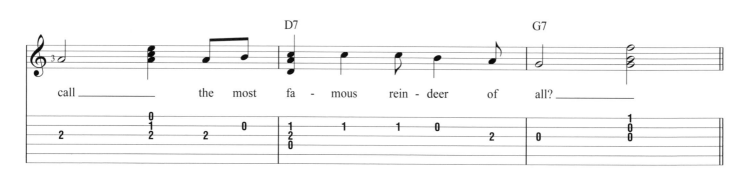

Strum Pattern: 2, 3
Pick Pattern: 2, 3

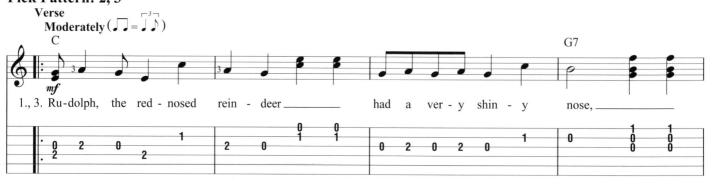

Copyright © 1958 (Renewed 1986) St. Nicholas Music Inc., 254 W. 54th Street, 12th Floor, New York, New York 10019
All Rights Reserved

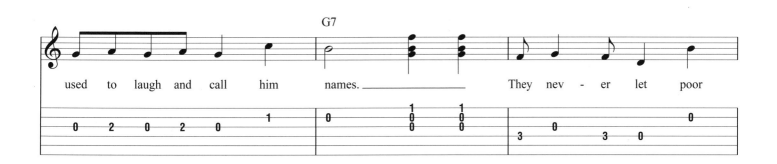

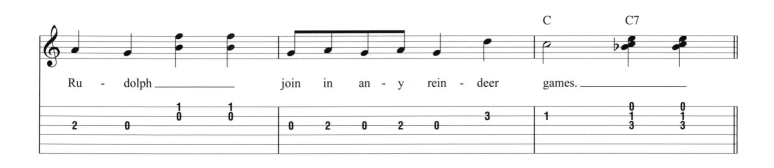

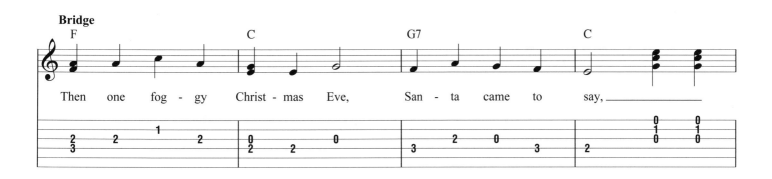

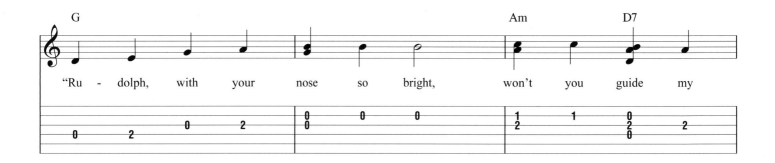

"Ru - dolph, with your nose so bright, won't you guide my

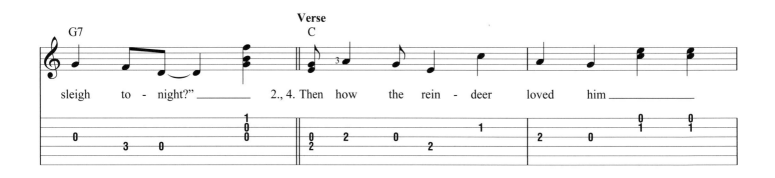

sleigh to - night?" _____ 2., 4. Then how the rein - deer loved him _____

as they shout - ed out with glee; _____ "Ru - dolph, the red - nosed

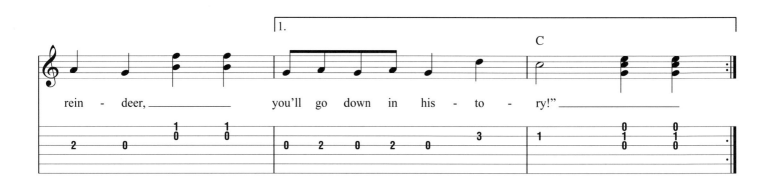

rein - deer, _____ you'll go down in his - to - ry!" _____

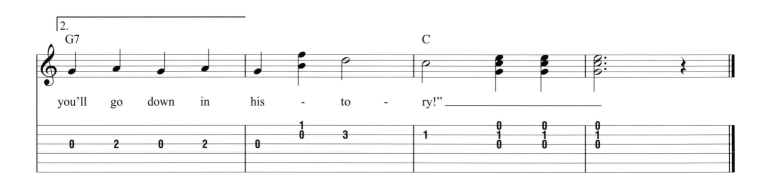

you'll go down in his - to - ry!" _____

Santa Baby

By Joan Javits, Phil Springer and Tony Springer

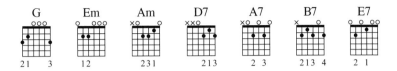

Strum Pattern: 1, 3
Pick Pattern: 2, 3

Intro
Moderately slow

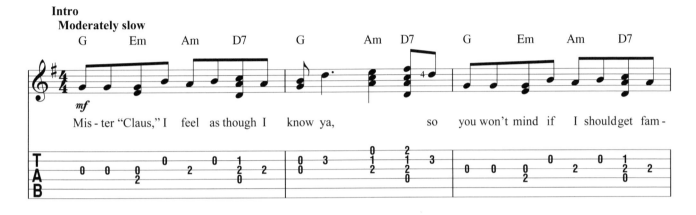

Mis - ter "Claus," I feel as though I know ya, so you won't mind if I should get fam -

Verse

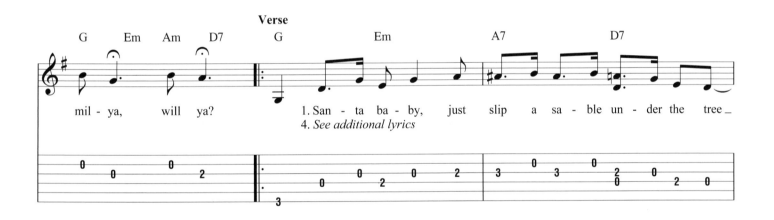

mil - ya, will ya?
1. San - ta ba - by, just slip a sa - ble un - der the tree _
4. *See additional lyrics*

for me; been an aw - ful good girl. _ San - ta ba - by, so

Copyright Renewed 1981 and Controlled in the U.S. by Philip Springer
Copyright Controlled for the world outside the U.S. by Alley Music Corp. and Trio Music Company
All Rights for Trio Music Company Administered by BMG Rights Management (US) LLC
International Copyright Secured   All Rights Reserved

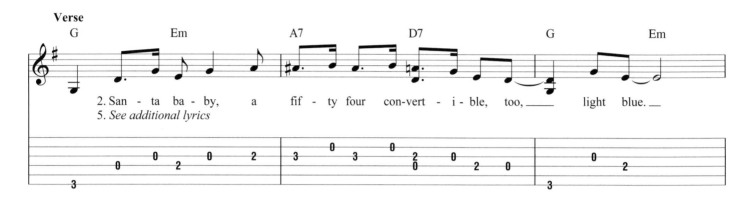

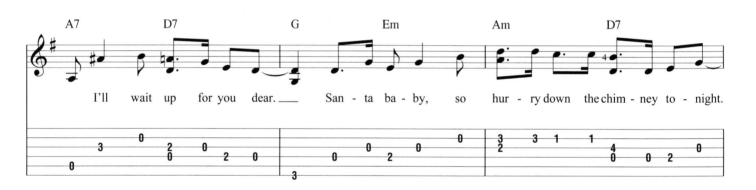

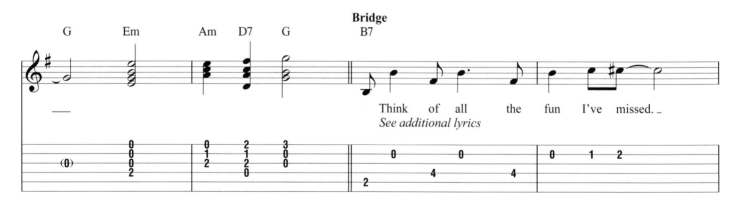

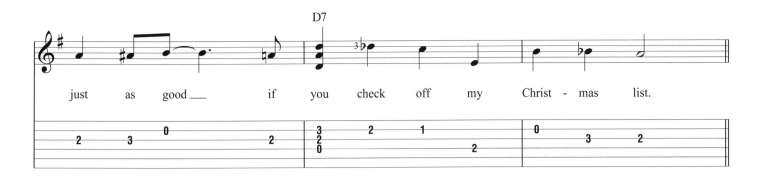

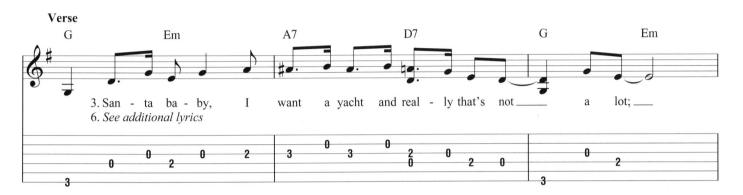

Verse

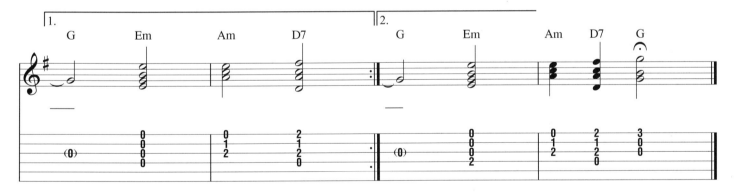

Additional Lyrics

4. Santa baby, one little thing I really do need:
   The deed to a platinum mine.
   Santa honey, so hurry down the chimney tonight.

5. Santa cutie, and fill my stocking with a duplex and cheques.
   Sign your X on the line.
   Santa cutie, and hurry down the chimney tonight.

Bridge   Come and trim my Christmas tree
   With some decorations at Tiffany.
   I really do believe in you.
   Let's see if you believe in me.

6. Santa baby, forgot to mention one little thing, a ring!
   I don't mean on the phone.
   Santa baby, so hurry down the chimney tonight.

Santa Claus Is Comin' to Town

Words by Haven Gillespie
Music by J. Fred Coots

Strum Pattern: 4
Pick Pattern: 4

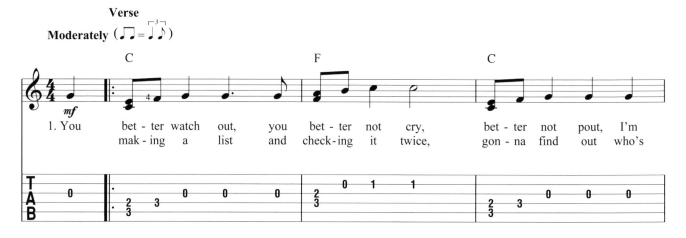

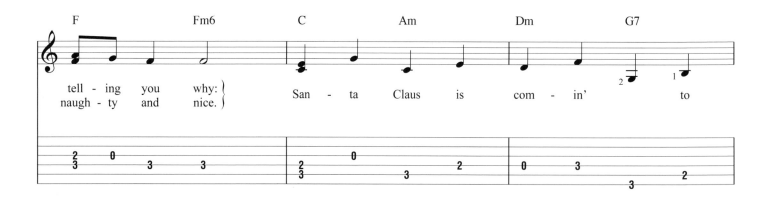

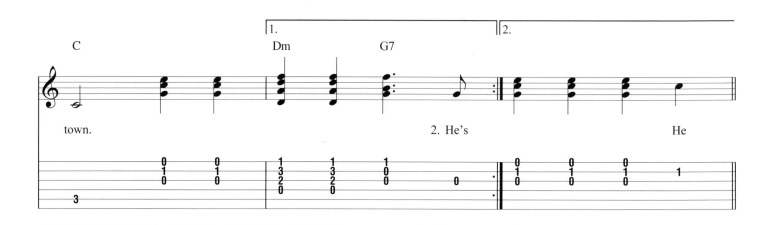

Copyright © 1934 Toy Town Tunes, Inc. and Haven Gillespie Music
Copyright Renewed
All Rights on behalf of Toy Town Tunes, Inc. Administered in the United States and Canada by Wixen Music Publishing, Inc.
All Rights Reserved   Used by Permissio

Bridge

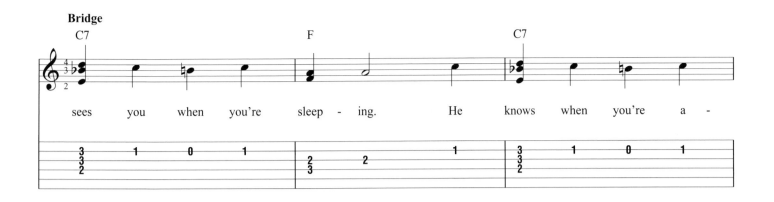

sees you when you're sleep - ing. He knows when you're a -

wake. He knows if you've been bad or good, so be

Outro-Verse

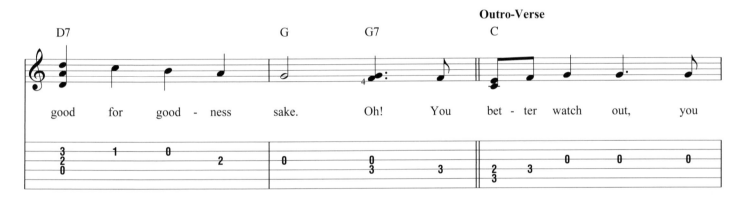

good for good - ness sake. Oh! You bet - ter watch out, you

bet - ter not cry, bet - ter not pout, I'm tell - ing you why:

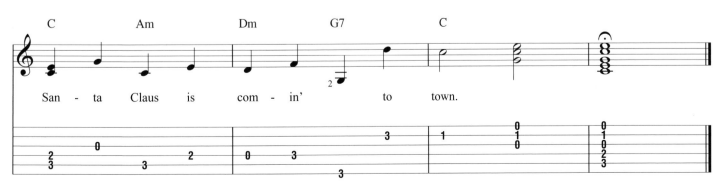

San - ta Claus is com - in' to town.

Silver Bells

from the Paramount Picture THE LEMON DROP KID

Words and Music by Jay Livingston and Ray Evans

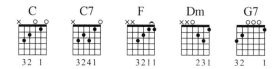

Strum Pattern: 9
Pick Pattern: 8

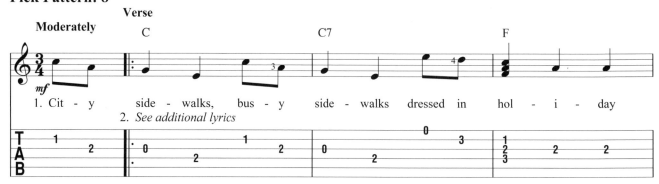

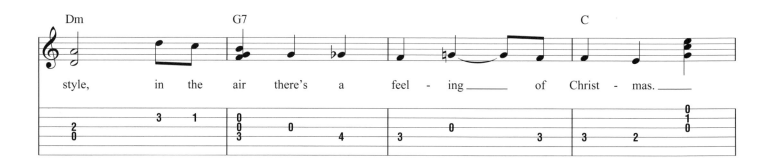

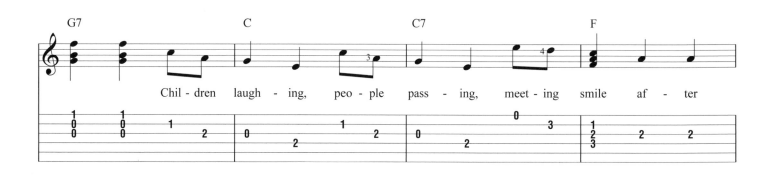

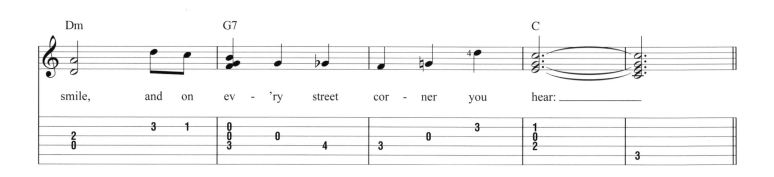

Copyright © 1950 Sony Music Publishing (US) LLC
Copyright Renewed
All Rights Administered by Sony Music Publishing (US) LLC, 424 Church Street, Suite 1200, Nashville, TN 37219
International Copyright Secured   All Rights Reserved

Chorus

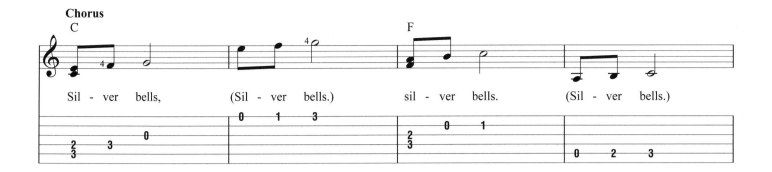

Sil - ver bells, (Sil - ver bells.) sil - ver bells. (Sil - ver bells.)

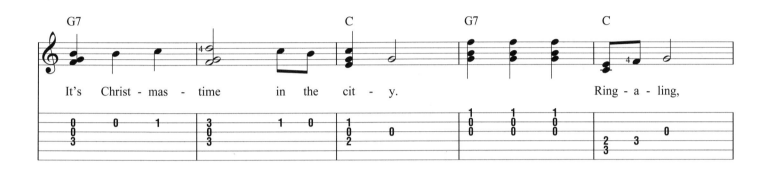

It's Christ - mas - time in the cit - y. Ring - a - ling,

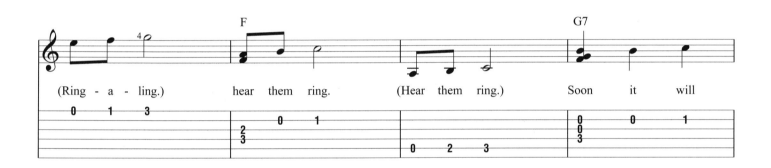

(Ring - a - ling.) hear them ring. (Hear them ring.) Soon it will

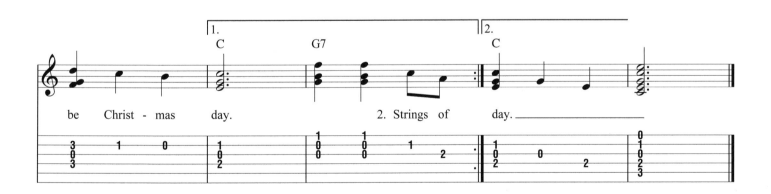

be Christ - mas day. 2. Strings of day.

Additional Lyrics

2. Strings of street lights, even stop lights
   Blink a bright red and green,
   As the shoppers rush home with their treasures.
   Hear the snow crunch, see the kids bunch,
   This is Santa's big scene,
   And above all the bustle you hear:

White Christmas

from the Motion Picture Irving Berlin's HOLIDAY INN
Words and Music by Irving Berlin

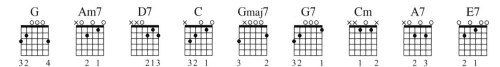

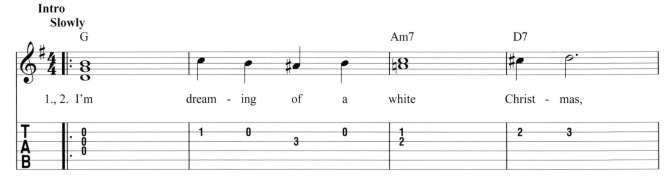

Strum Pattern: 3
Pick Pattern: 3

Intro
Slowly

1., 2. I'm dream - ing of a white Christ - mas,

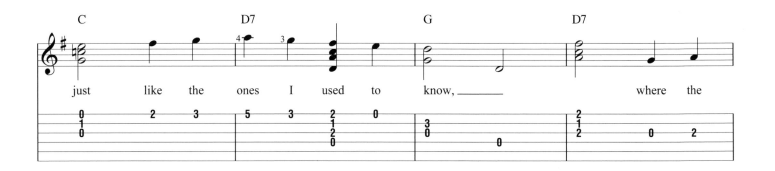

just like the ones I used to know, _____ where the

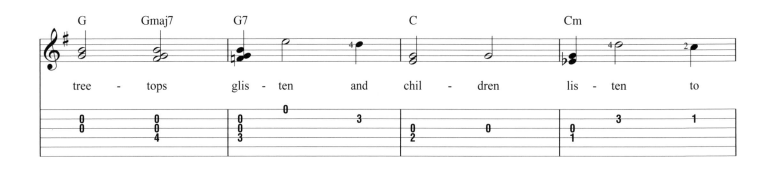

tree - tops glis - ten and chil - dren lis - ten to

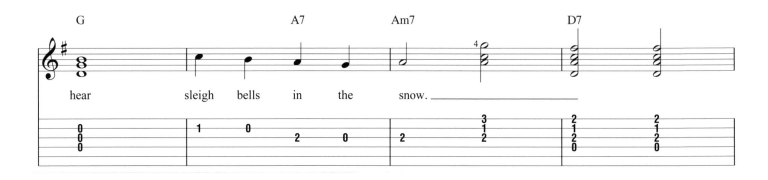

hear sleigh bells in the snow. _____

© Copyright 1940, 1942 by Irving Berlin
Copyright Renewed
International Copyright Secured   All Rights Reserved

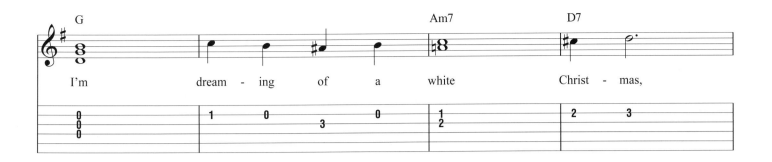

I'm dream - ing of a white Christ - mas,

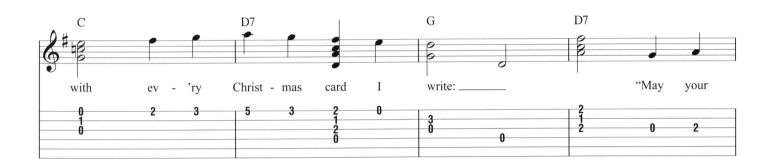

with ev - 'ry Christ - mas card I write: _____ "May your

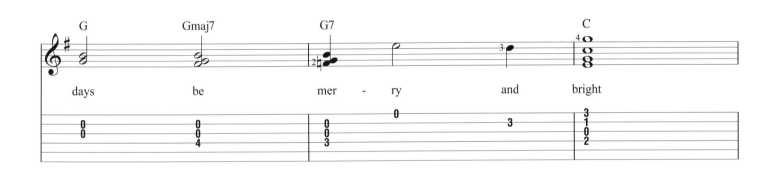

days be mer - ry and bright

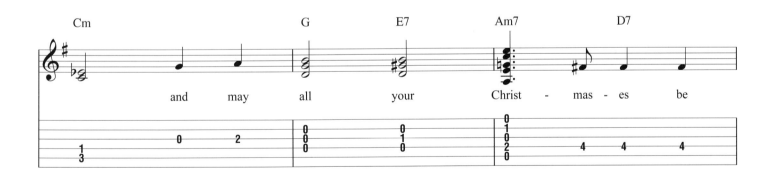

and may all your Christ - mas - es be

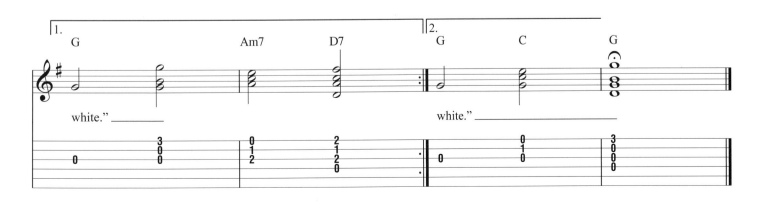

1.

white." _____

2.

white." _____

Winter Wonderland

Words by Dick Smith
Music by Felix Bernard

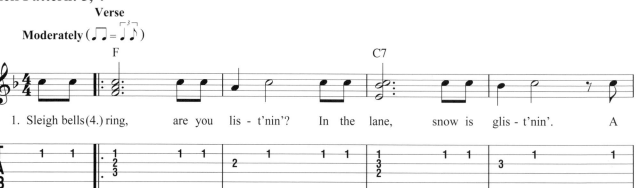

Strum Pattern: 3, 4
Pick Pattern: 3, 4

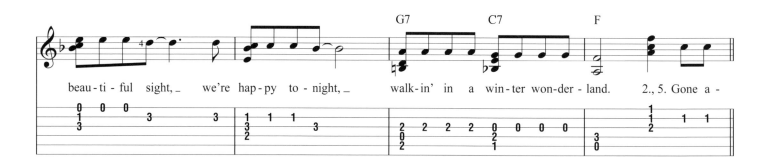

1. Sleigh bells (4.) ring, are you lis - t'nin'? In the lane, snow is glis - t'nin'. A

beau - ti - ful sight, _ we're hap - py to - night, _ walk - in' in a win - ter won - der - land. 2., 5. Gone a -

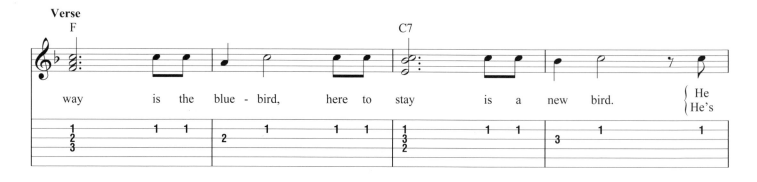

Verse

way is the blue - bird, here to stay is a new bird. He / He's

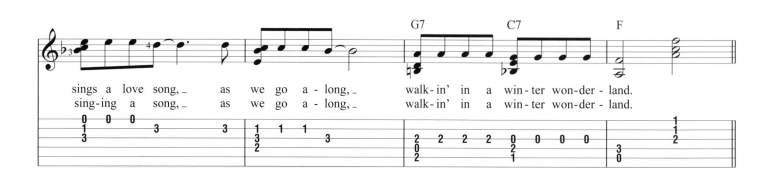

sings a love song, _ as we go a - long, _ walk - in' in a win - ter won - der - land.
sing - ing a song, _ as we go a - long, _ walk - in' in a win - ter won - der - land.

© 1934 (Renewed) WC MUSIC CORP.
All Rights for the Dick Smith share in Canada Administered by REDWOOD MUSIC LTD.
All Rights Reserved Used by Permission

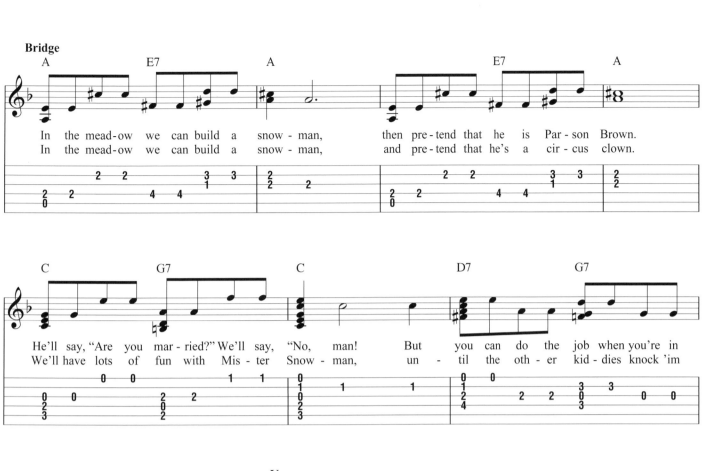

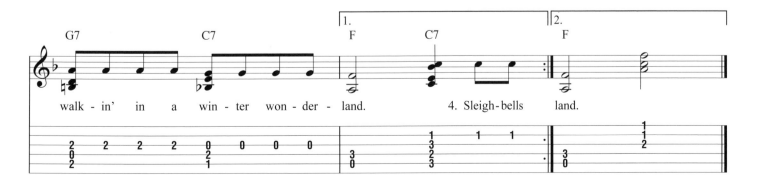

Wonderful Christmastime

Words and Music by Paul McCartney

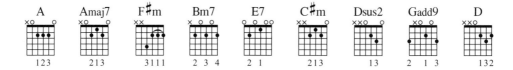

Strum Pattern: 2
Pick Pattern: 4

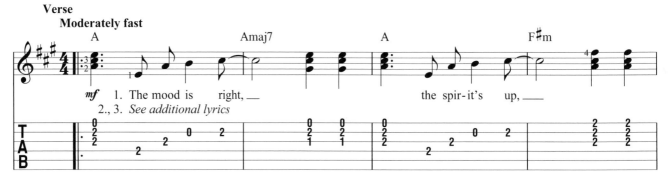

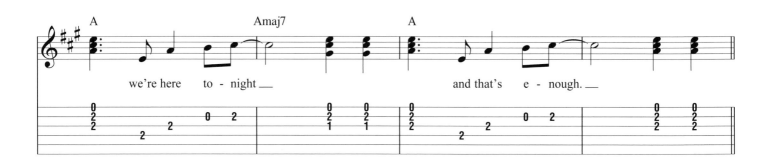

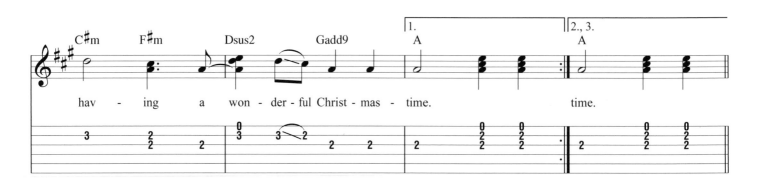

© 1979 MPL COMMUNICATIONS LTD.
Administered by MPL COMMUNICATIONS, INC.
All Rights Reserved

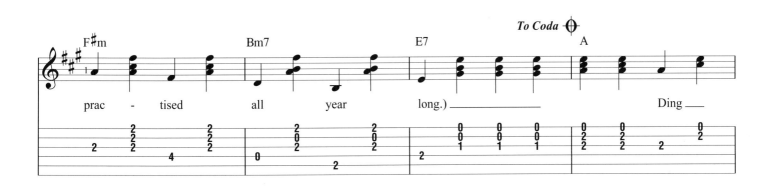

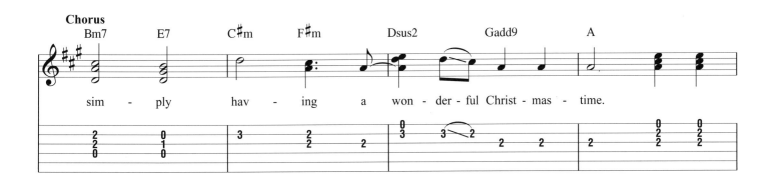

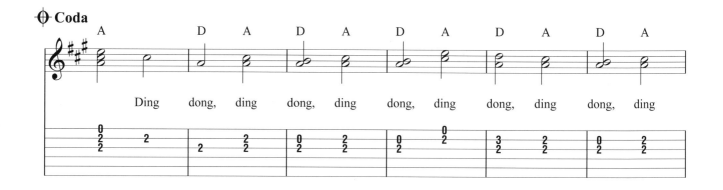

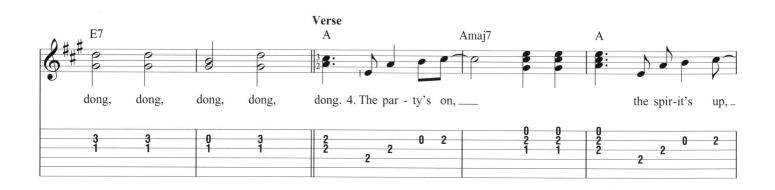

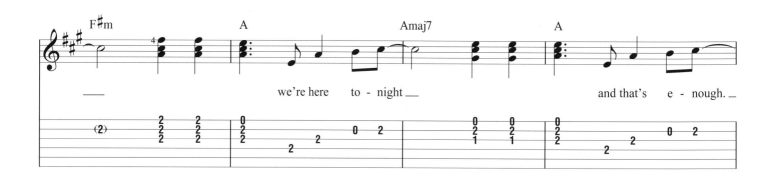

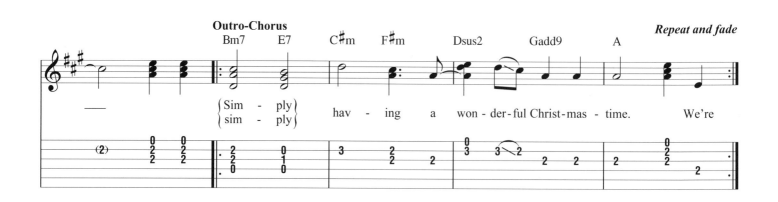

Additional Lyrics

2. The party's on,
   The feeling's here
   That only comes
   This time of year.

3. The word is out
   About the town,
   To lift a glass.
   Oh, don't look down.

Celebrate Christmas
WITH YOUR GUITAR AND HAL LEONARD

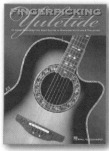

THE BEST CHRISTMAS GUITAR FAKE BOOK EVER

Over 150 Christmas classics for guitar. Songs include: Blue Christmas • The Chipmunk Song • Frosty the Snow Man • Happy Holiday • A Holly Jolly Christmas • I Saw Mommy Kissing Santa Claus • I Wonder As I Wander • Jingle-Bell Rock • Rudolph, the Red-Nosed Reindeer • Santa Bring My Baby Back (To Me) • Suzy Snowflake • Tennessee Christmas • and more.
00240053 Melody/Lyrics/Chords...........$29.99

THE BIG CHRISTMAS COLLECTION FOR EASY GUITAR

Includes over 70 Christmas favorites, such as: Ave Maria • Blue Christmas • Deck the Hall • Feliz Navidad • Frosty the Snow Man • Happy Holiday • A Holly Jolly Christmas • Joy to the World • O Holy Night • Silver and Gold • Suzy Snowflake • and more. Does not include TAB.
00698978 Easy Guitar $19.99

CHRISTMAS CAROLS
For Easy Guitar

24 holiday favorites, including: Carol of the Bells • Good King Wenceslas • Hark! the Herald Angels Sing • I Saw Three Ships • Jingle Bells • Jolly Old St. Nicholas • O Come, O Come Immanuel • O Little Town of Bethlehem • Up on the Housetop • and more. Does not include TAB.
00702221 Easy Guitar $10.99

CHRISTMAS CAROLS
Guitar Chord Songbook

80 favorite carols for guitarists who just need the lyrics and chords: Angels We Have Heard on High • Away in a Manger • Deck the Hall • Good King Wenceslas • The Holly and the Ivy • Irish Carol • Jingle Bells • Joy to the World • O Holy Night • Rocking • Silent Night • Up on the Housetop • Welsh Carol • What Child Is This? • and more.
00699536 Lyrics/Chord Symbols/
        Guitar Chord Diagrams $14.99

CLASSICAL GUITAR CHRISTMAS SHEET MUSIC

30 top holiday songs: Away in a Manger • Deck the Hall • Go, Tell It on the Mountain • Hallelujah Chorus • I Saw Three Ships • Jingle Bells • O Little Town of Bethlehem • Silent Night • The Twelve Days of Christmas • Up on the Housetop • We Wish You a Merry Christmas • What Child Is This? • and more. Does not include TAB.
00146974 Solo Classical Guitar $10.99

CHRISTMAS JAZZ

Jazz Guitar Chord Melody Solos

21 songs in chord-melody style for the beginning to intermediate jazz guitarist in standard notation and tablature: Auld Lang Syne • Baby, It's Cold Outside • Cool Yule • Have Yourself a Merry Little Christmas • Mary, Did You Know? • Santa Baby • White Christmas • Winter Wonderland • and more.
00171334 Solo Guitar...........................$15.99

CHRISTMAS SONGS FOR EASY GUITAR

20 classic Christmas tunes: Blue Christmas • The Christmas Song (Chestnuts Roasting) • Frosty the Snow Man • Christmas Time Is Here • A Holly Jolly Christmas • I Saw Mommy Kissing Santa Claus • I'll Be Home for Christmas • Jingle-Bell Rock • Merry Christmas, Darling • Rudolph the Red-Nosed Reindeer • Silver Bells • You're All I Want for Christmas • and more.
00699804 Easy Guitar $9.99

FINGERPICKING CHRISTMAS SONGS

15 songs for intermediate-level guitarists, combining melody and harmony in superb fingerpicking arrangements: Baby, It's Cold Outside • Caroling, Caroling • Have Yourself a Merry Little Christmas • I Heard the Bells on Christmas Day • The Little Drummer Boy • Mary, Did You Know? • Mele Kalikimaka • Sleigh Ride • White Christmas • Wonderful Christmastime • and more.
00171333 Fingerstyle Guitar..................$10.99

FINGERPICKING YULETIDE

Carefully written for intermediate-level guitarists, this collection includes an introduction to fingerstyle guitar and 16 holiday favorites: Do You Hear What I Hear • Happy Xmas (War Is Over) • A Holly Jolly Christmas • Jingle-Bell Rock • Rudolph the Red-Nosed Reindeer • and more.
00699654 Fingerstyle Guitar..................$12.99

FIRST 50 CHRISTMAS CAROLS YOU SHOULD PLAY ON GUITAR

Accessible, must-know Christmas songs are included in this collection arranged for guitar solo with a combo of tab, chords and lyrics. Includes: Angels We Have Heard on High • The First Noel • God Rest Ye Merry, Gentlemen • The Holly and the Ivy • O Christmas Tree • Silent Night • Up on the Housetop • What Child Is This? • and more.
00236224 Guitar Solo...........................$12.99

3-CHORD CHRISTMAS

You only need to know how to play 3 chords (G, C and D) on guitar to master these 25 holiday favorites: Away in a Manger • The Chipmunk Song • Frosty the Snow Man • Go, Tell It on the Mountain • Here Comes Santa Claus • Jingle Bells • The Little Drummer Boy • O Christmas Tree • Silent Night • Silver Bells • While Shepherds Watched Their Flocks • and more.
00146973 Guitar Solo...........................$10.99

THE ULTIMATE GUITAR CHRISTMAS FAKE BOOK

200 Christmas standards: All I Want for Christmas Is You • Baby, It's Cold Outside • The Christmas Song (Chestnuts Roasting on an Open Fire) • Do You Want to Build a Snowman? • Feliz Navidad • Frosty the Snow Man • A Holly Jolly Christmas • Jingle Bells • Let It Snow! Let It Snow! Let It Snow! • Mary, Did You Know? • Rockin' Around the Christmas Tree • Santa Baby • Silent Night • What Child Is This? • White Christmas • and more.
00236446 Melody/Lyrics/Chords..........$29.99

HAL•LEONARD®
www.halleonard.com

Prices, contents and availability subject to change without notice.

EASY GUITAR WITH NOTES & TAB

This series features simplified arrangements with notes, tab, chord charts, and strum and pick patterns.

MIXED FOLIOS

00702287	Acoustic	$19.99
00702002	Acoustic Rock Hits for Easy Guitar	$15.99
00702166	All-Time Best Guitar Collection	$19.99
00702232	Best Acoustic Songs for Easy Guitar	$16.99
00119835	Best Children's Songs	$16.99
00703055	The Big Book of Nursery Rhymes & Children's Songs	$16.99
00698978	Big Christmas Collection	$19.99
00702394	Bluegrass Songs for Easy Guitar	$15.99
00289632	Bohemian Rhapsody	$19.99
00703387	Celtic Classics	$16.99
00224808	Chart Hits of 2016-2017	$14.99
00267383	Chart Hits of 2017-2018	$14.99
00334293	Chart Hits of 2019-2020	$16.99
00403479	Chart Hits of 2021-2022	$16.99
00702149	Children's Christian Songbook	$9.99
00702028	Christmas Classics	$8.99
00101779	Christmas Guitar	$14.99
00702141	Classic Rock	$8.95
00159642	Classical Melodies	$12.99
00253933	Disney/Pixar's Coco	$16.99
00702203	CMT's 100 Greatest Country Songs	$34.99
00702283	The Contemporary Christian Collection	$16.99

00196954	Contemporary Disney	$19.99
00702239	Country Classics for Easy Guitar	$24.99
00702257	Easy Acoustic Guitar Songs	$17.99
00702041	Favorite Hymns for Easy Guitar	$12.99
00222701	Folk Pop Songs	$17.99
00126894	Frozen	$14.99
00333922	Frozen 2	$14.99
00702286	Glee	$16.99
00702160	The Great American Country Songbook	$19.99
00702148	Great American Gospel for Guitar	$14.99
00702050	Great Classical Themes for Easy Guitar	$9.99
00275088	The Greatest Showman	$17.99
00148030	Halloween Guitar Songs	$14.99
00702273	Irish Songs	$14.99
00192503	Jazz Classics for Easy Guitar	$16.99
00702275	Jazz Favorites for Easy Guitar	$17.99
00702274	Jazz Standards for Easy Guitar	$19.99
00702162	Jumbo Easy Guitar Songbook	$24.99
00232285	La La Land	$16.99
00702258	Legends of Rock	$14.99
00702189	MTV's 100 Greatest Pop Songs	$34.99
00702272	1950s Rock	$16.99
00702271	1960s Rock	$16.99
00702270	1970s Rock	$24.99
00702269	1980s Rock	$16.99

00702268	1990s Rock	$24.99
00369043	Rock Songs for Kids	$14.99
00109725	Once	$14.99
00702187	Selections from O Brother Where Art Thou?	$19.99
00702178	100 Songs for Kids	$16.99
00702515	Pirates of the Caribbean	$17.99
00702125	Praise and Worship for Guitar	$14.99
00287930	Songs from *A Star Is Born, The Greatest Showman, La La Land*, and More Movie Musicals	$16.99
00702285	Southern Rock Hits	$12.99
00156420	Star Wars Music	$16.99
00121535	30 Easy Celtic Guitar Solos	$16.99
00244654	Top Hits of 2017	$14.99
00283786	Top Hits of 2018	$14.99
00302269	Top Hits of 2019	$14.99
00355779	Top Hits of 2020	$14.99
00374083	Top Hits of 2021	$16.99
00702294	Top Worship Hits	$17.99
00702255	VH1's 100 Greatest Hard Rock Songs	$34.99
00702175	VH1's 100 Greatest Songs of Rock and Roll	$34.99
00702253	Wicked	$12.99

ARTIST COLLECTIONS

00702267	AC/DC for Easy Guitar	$16.99
00156221	Adele – 25	$16.99
00396889	Adele – 30	$19.99
00702040	Best of the Allman Brothers	$16.99
00702865	J.S. Bach for Easy Guitar	$15.99
00702169	Best of The Beach Boys	$16.99
00702292	The Beatles — 1	$22.99
00125796	Best of Chuck Berry	$16.99
00702201	The Essential Black Sabbath	$15.99
00702250	blink-182 — Greatest Hits	$17.99
02501615	Zac Brown Band — The Foundation	$17.99
02501621	Zac Brown Band — You Get What You Give	$16.99
00702043	Best of Johnny Cash	$17.99
00702090	Eric Clapton's Best	$16.99
00702086	Eric Clapton — from the Album Unplugged	$17.99
00702202	The Essential Eric Clapton	$17.99
00702053	Best of Patsy Cline	$17.99
00222697	Very Best of Coldplay – 2nd Edition	$17.99
00702229	The Very Best of Creedence Clearwater Revival	$16.99
00702145	Best of Jim Croce	$16.99
00702278	Crosby, Stills & Nash	$12.99
14042809	Bob Dylan	$15.99
00702276	Fleetwood Mac — Easy Guitar Collection	$17.99
00139462	The Very Best of Grateful Dead	$16.99
00702136	Best of Merle Haggard	$16.99
00702227	Jimi Hendrix — Smash Hits	$19.99
00702288	Best of Hillsong United	$12.99
00702236	Best of Antonio Carlos Jobim	$15.99

00702245	Elton John — Greatest Hits 1970–2002	$19.99
00129855	Jack Johnson	$17.99
00702204	Robert Johnson	$16.99
00702234	Selections from Toby Keith — 35 Biggest Hits	$12.95
00702003	Kiss	$16.99
00702216	Lynyrd Skynyrd	$17.99
00702182	The Essential Bob Marley	$16.99
00146081	Maroon 5	$14.99
00121925	Bruno Mars – Unorthodox Jukebox	$12.99
00702248	Paul McCartney — All the Best	$14.99
00125484	The Best of MercyMe	$12.99
00702209	Steve Miller Band — Young Hearts (Greatest Hits)	$12.95
00124167	Jason Mraz	$15.99
00702096	Best of Nirvana	$16.99
00702211	The Offspring — Greatest Hits	$17.99
00138026	One Direction	$17.99
00702030	Best of Roy Orbison	$17.99
00702144	Best of Ozzy Osbourne	$14.99
00702279	Tom Petty	$17.99
00102911	Pink Floyd	$17.99
00702139	Elvis Country Favorites	$19.99
00702293	The Very Best of Prince	$19.99
00699415	Best of Queen for Guitar	$16.99
00109279	Best of R.E.M.	$14.99
00702208	Red Hot Chili Peppers — Greatest Hits	$17.99
00198960	The Rolling Stones	$17.99
00174793	The Very Best of Santana	$16.99
00702196	Best of Bob Seger	$16.99
00146046	Ed Sheeran	$17.99

00702252	Frank Sinatra — Nothing But the Best	$12.99
00702010	Best of Rod Stewart	$17.99
00702049	Best of George Strait	$17.99
00702259	Taylor Swift for Easy Guitar	$15.99
00359800	Taylor Swift – Easy Guitar Anthology	$24.99
00702260	Taylor Swift — Fearless	$14.99
00139727	Taylor Swift — 1989	$19.99
00115960	Taylor Swift — Red	$16.99
00253667	Taylor Swift — Reputation	$17.99
00702290	Taylor Swift — Speak Now	$16.99
00232849	Chris Tomlin Collection – 2nd Edition	$14.99
00702226	Chris Tomlin — See the Morning	$12.95
00148643	Train	$14.99
00702427	U2 — 18 Singles	$19.99
00702108	Best of Stevie Ray Vaughan	$17.99
00279005	The Who	$14.99
00702123	Best of Hank Williams	$15.99
00194548	Best of John Williams	$14.99
00702228	Neil Young — Greatest Hits	$17.99
00119133	Neil Young — Harvest	$14.99

Prices, contents and availability subject to change without notice.

HAL•LEONARD®

Visit Hal Leonard online at **halleonard.com**